Thomas Secker, Beilby Porteus, George Stinton

Eight charges delivered to the clergy of the dioceses of Oxford and Canterbury

Fourth Edition

Thomas Secker, Beilby Porteus, George Stinton

Eight charges delivered to the clergy of the dioceses of Oxford and Canterbury
Fourth Edition

ISBN/EAN: 9783337142889

Printed in Europe, USA, Canada, Australia, Japan

Cover: Foto ©Andreas Hilbeck / pixelio.de

More available books at **www.hansebooks.com**

EIGHT CHARGES

DELIVERED TO THE

CLERGY

OF THE DIOCESES OF

OXFORD AND CANTERBURY.

TO WHICH ARE ADDED

INSTRUCTIONS

TO

CANDIDATES FOR ORDERS;

AND A

LATIN SPEECH

Intended to have been made at the Opening of the CONVOCATION in 1761.

By THOMAS SECKER, LL. D.
Late LORD ARCHBISHOP OF CANTERBURY.

Published from the Original Manuscripts,
By BEILBY PORTEUS, D.D. and GEORGE STINTON, D.D.
His Grace's Chaplains.

THE FOURTH EDITION.

LONDON:
Printed for JOHN, FRANCIS and CHARLES RIVINGTON,
N° 62, St. Paul's Church yard; and BENJAMIN WHITE
and SON, in Fleet street. 1790.

CONTENTS.

THE Bishop of Oxford's Charge to his Clergy in the Year 1738, Page 3

The Bishop of Oxford's Charge to his Clergy in the Year 1741, 47

The Bishop of Oxford's Charge to his Clergy in the Year 1747, 87

The Bishop of Oxford's Charge to his Clergy in the Year 1750, 123

The Bishop of Oxford's Charge to his Clergy in the Year 1753, 165

The Archbishop of Canterbury's Charge to his Clergy in the Year 1758, 205

The Archbishop of Canterbury's Charge to his Clergy in the Year 1762, 245

The Archbishop of Canterbury's Charge to his Clergy in the Year 1766, 287

Instructions given to Candidates for Orders after their subscribing the Articles, 327

Oratio quam coram Synodo Provinciæ Cantuariensis anno 1761 convocatâ habendam scripserat, sed morbo præpeditus non habuit, Archiepiscopus, 349

LATELY PUBLISHED,

By JOHN RIVINGTON and SONS, in St. Paul's Church-yard; and BENJAMIN WHITE and SON, in Fleet-Street;

I. Archbishop SECKER's Lectures on the Catechism, in Two Vols. Octavo, Seventh Edition, Price 12s. bound.

II. Archbishop SECKER's Sermons on several Occasions; to which is prefixed, A Review of his Grace's Life and Character. In Seven Vols. Octavo, Price 2l. 2s.

The above Nine Volumes were published from the original Manuscripts, by his Grace's Chaplains, BEILBY PORTEUS, *D.D. now Lord Bishop of London, and* GEORGE STINTON, *D.D.*

III. Archbishop SECKER's Nine Sermons preached in the Parish of *St. James, Westminster*, on Occasion of the War and Rebellion in 1745. Published in his Grace's Life-time. To which are added, His Grace's Answer to Dr. MAYHEW, and his Letter to Mr. HORATIO WALPOLE. The Third Edition, Price 6s.

IV. Archbishop SECKER's Fourteen Sermons on several Occasions. Published in his Grace's Life-time. The Second Edition, in one Vol. Octavo, Price 6s.

☞ The above mentioned Eleven Vols. with these Charges, compleat his Grace's Works in Twelve Vols. Octavo, Price 3l. 12s. neatly bound.

THE
CHARGE

OF

THOMAS Lord Bishop of OXFORD

TO THE

CLERGY of the DIOCESE,

IN

His PRIMARY VISITATION 1738.

Published at Their REQUEST.

THE SEVENTH EDITION.

A

Reverend Brethren,

I AM very senfible, that you cannot meet together on this Occafion, without making deep Reflections on the Lofs, which you have fuffered, for the public Good, by the Removal of a Paftor, whom the Experience of fo many Years hath taught you to efteem and honour fo highly. It is your farther Unhappinefs, that He is fucceeded by a Perfon, very unequal to the Care of this confpicuous and important Diocefe. But your Humanity and your Piety will, I doubt not, incline you, both to accept and to affift the Endeavours of one, who can affure you, with very great Truth, that he is earneftly defirous of being as ufeful to you all, as he can; and ferioufly concerned for the Interefts of Religion, and of this Church. Would to God there were lefs Need of expressing a Concern for them, than there is at present!

Men have always complained of their own Times: and always with too much Reason. But though it is natural to think those Evils the greatest, which we feel ourselves; and therefore Mistakes are easily made, in comparing one Age with another: yet in this we cannot be mistaken, that an open and professed Disregard to Religion is become, through a Variety of unhappy Causes, the distinguishing Character of the present Age; that this Evil is grown to a great Height in the Metropolis of the Nation; is daily spreading through every Part of it; and, bad in itself as any can be, must of Necessity bring in most others after it. Indeed it hath already brought in such Dissoluteness and Contempt of Principle in the higher Part of the World, and such profligate Intemperance, and Fearlessness of committing Crimes, in the lower, as must, if this Torrent of Impiety stop not, become absolutely fatal. And God knows, far from stopping, it receives, through the ill Designs of some Persons, and the Inconsiderateness of others, a continual a continual Increase. Christianity is now ridiculed and railed at, with very little Reserve: and the Teachers of it, without any at all. Indeed with Respect to Us, the Rule, which most of our Adversaries appear to have set themselves, is, to be, at all Adventures, as bitter as they can: and they follow it, not only beyond Truth, but beyond Probability: asserting the very worst Things of us without Foundation, and exaggerating every Thing without Mercy: imputing the Faults, and sometimes imaginary Faults, of particular Persons to the whole Order; and then declaiming against us all promiscuously with such wild Vehemence, as, in any Case but ours, they themselves would think, in the highest Degree, unjust and cruel. Or if sometimes a few Exceptions are made, they are usually made only to divide us amongst ourselves: to deceive one Part of us, and throw a greater Odium upon the other. Still, were these Invectives only to affect Us personally, dear as our Reputations are and ought to be to us, the Mischief would be small, in comparison of what it is. But the Consequence hath been, as it naturally must, that Disregard to Us hath greatly increased the Disregard to public Worship and Instruction: that many are grown prejudiced against Religion; many more, indifferent about it and unacquainted with it. And the Emissaries of the *Romish* Church, taking the Members of ours at this unhappy Disadvantage, have begun to reap great Harvests in the Field, which hath been thus prepared for them by the Labours of those, who would be thought their most irreconcileable Enemies.

Yet, however melancholy the View before us appears, we have no Reason to be discouraged: for let us take Care of our Duty, and God will take Care of the Event. But we have great Reason to think seriously, what our Duty on this Occasion is; and stir up each other to the Performance of it: that where-ever the Guilt of these Things may fall, it must not fall on our heads. *For it must needs be, that Offences come: but wo to that Man, by whom the Offence cometh*[*]. Our Grief for the Decay of Religion might be attended with much Comfort in Regard to

[*] Matth. xviii. 7.

ourselves,

ourselves, could we but truly say, that no Faults or Infirmities of ours had ever given Advantages against it. But though, God be thanked, we are far from being what our Adversaries would represent us; whose Reproaches perhaps were never less deserved, than now when they are the most violent: yet, it must be owned, we are not by any Means, even the best of us, what we ought to be. And the present State of Things calls loudly upon us, to correct our Mistakes, to supply our Deficiencies, and to do all we are able for the Honour of God, and the Happiness of Mankind.

If we can be unconcerned now, we have neither Piety nor common Prudence in us. And if we are concerned in Earnest, we shall be very desirous, both to avoid all wrong Methods of shewing it, and to make use of all right ones.

Complaining of our Superiors for those Evils, which perhaps they cannot prevent; or complaining of them with Disrespect, for what we may apprehend they could prevent, would both be undutiful and imprudent Conduct: would give our Adversaries

Joy, and do our Cause Harm. Indeed to beg earnestly of God, that He would direct the Hearts of those, who preside over the public Welfare; and humbly to represent to them, on all fit Occasions, the declining State of Religion, the Importance and the Means of preserving it; these Things are unquestionable Duties. But then we must always approve ourselves, at the same Time, conscientiously loyal both in Word and deed; reasonable in our Expectations; sincerely grateful for the Protection, which we are assured of enjoying; and duly sensible, that every Thing of Value to us, in this World, depends on the Support of that Government, under which we now live. We cannot be good Men, if we are bad Subjects; and we are not wise Men, if we permit ourselves to be suspected of it.

A second proper Caution is, That to speak unfavourably of Liberty, religious or civil, instead of carefully distinguishing both from the many Abuses of them, which we daily see; or to encourage any other Restraints on either, than public Utility makes evidently needful; can only serve to increase that

Jealousy, which, being in former Ages grounded too well, hath been most industriously heightened, when there never was so little Pretence of Ground for it; that the Claims of the Clergy are hurtful to the Rights of Mankind. It concerns us greatly to remove so dangerous a Prejudice against us, as this: not by renouncing those Powers, which the Gospel hath given us; for we are bound to assert them: but by convincing the World, that they are perfectly innocent; and avoiding all Appearance of assuming what we have no Right to: by shewing our Abhorrence of Tyranny, especially over the Consciences of Men; and satisfying them fully, if possible, that *we preach not ourselves, but Christ Jesus, the Lord; and ourselves, their Servants for his Sake*[b]. Then, with Respect to the Privileges, that we derive from human Authority: as, on the one Hand, receding from any of them without Cause is only inviting fresh Encroachments, and giving needless Advantages to such as will be sure to lose none: so, on the other, straining them too far is the likeliest Way

[b] 2 Cor. iv. 5.

to destroy them all at once: and both our Usefulness and our Security depend very much, on our appearing plainly to desire nothing inconsistent with the common Good; to have the truest Concern for all reasonable Liberty, and to be zealous only against Licentiousness and Confusion.

Thirdly, If we should be tempted to oppose Profaneness, by encouraging the opposite Extreme of Superstition: this also would be unjustifiable in itself; would have bad Effects upon as many as we might mislead; and give great Opportunities to all that should see them misled, either of accusing Religion, or exposing us, as Corrupters of Religion. Not that we are to give up inconsiderately, whatever some Persons are pleased to charge with Superstition: for there would be no End of Concessions at that Rate: but only to avoid encouraging any Thing, that can be justly charged with it; and then we shall stand upon sure Ground. For nothing can be more unjust, than those Imputations of it, which our Adversaries are so fond of throwing, some upon Christianity itself, others on the Doctrine and Worship of that

that Church, of which, through God's merciful Providence, we have the Happiness to be Members.

Another very pernicious Error would be, if we should think to serve our Cause by intemperate Warmth in it. Christian Zeal indeed is a Duty, that never was more needful, and never less shewn. But Passion will do no Good. If expressed against those, who are indifferent about Religion, it will turn them into Enemies: if against the Enemies of Religion, it will make them yet more vehement Enemies. Besides, the extravagant Things, that Men say and attempt against us and our Profession, are not always designed Injuries; but frequently the Effects of Misrepresentations, and Prejudices, that have imperceptibly taken hold on Persons, who otherwise mean tolerably well. Now Mildness to such as these, is but Justice: and to all others, it is Prudence. Railing is the Province, which our Adversaries have chosen: and let us leave it to them. For whatever Success They may meet with that Way, as indeed they excel in it, We shall meet with none: but only make the Spirit

of

of Christianity be misunderstood and ill spoken of, by our own Want of it. Therefore, how injuriously soever we may be treated, let us return neither Injuries nor harsh Treatment for it: nor endeavour to mark out those Persons for Objects of popular Hatred, who are ever so unwearied in labouring to make Us so. Yet, at the same Time we must never court irreligious Men by wrong Compliances; never contribute to increase their Power of doing Harm; never desert our Duty, either for Fear of them, or Favour from them. But then let us defend both Religion and ourselves, with that Fairness and Decency, as well as Courage, which becomes our Function: acknowledge ingenuously whatever can be alledged against us with Truth, only claiming equitable Allowances; and where Charges are untrue, yet use mild Expostulations, not Reproaches; and try to shame our Opposers by the Reasonableness of what we say, rather than exasperate them by the Vehemence of it. They indeed have little Cause either to complain or to triumph, if, under such gross Provocations as they give, our Tempers sometimes

times fails: but we have great Cause to do our utmost, that it fail not.

And if undue Severity of Speech must be forborn towards professed Enemies; much more to those, who may, for aught we know, design themselves for Friends. Indeed, when it is evident, that Men only put on a Pretence of wishing well to Christianity, or the Teachers of it; and, whilst they affect to charge us with Uncharitableness for questioning their Sincerity, would despise us for believing them: there we must be allowed to see what plainly appears; and to speak of them, both as Adversaries, and unfair ones. Or when Doctrines, whatever the Intention of propagating them be, are inconsistent either with the Whole or any Part of our Religion; it is no Uncharitableness, but our Duty, to lay open the Falshood and the Danger of them. Nay, supposing only the legal Establishment of Religion, or some Branch of it, be attacked; yet the Attempt may both be injurious enough to Us, and detrimental enough to the Public, to deserve a vigorous Opposition. But to shew Passion and Bitterness in any of these Cases; to take

Pleasure

Pleasure in making Mens Mistakes or Designs thought worse than they are; to judge harshly of them with Respect to another World, or expose them to ill Usage in this; to refuse them due Allowances for human Infirmity, or be more backward to own their Merits, than to see their Faults: such Behaviour, instead of promoting Truth, will prejudice the World against it; will give Unbelievers dreadful Advantages, and for ever prevent that Union amongst Christians, which would procure us, above all Things, the Esteem of Men, and the Blessing of God.

From these improper Methods of supporting Religion, let us now proceed to the proper ones. And they will naturally fall under the general Heads, of our Instructions and our Lives.

Giving Instruction requires Knowledge. And therefore, as a competent Degree of it is justly expected of Persons, before they enter into Holy Orders: so, when they enter, the Care of making a continual Progress in it is solemnly promised by them, and covenanted for with them. What may be a very good Beginning, is by no Means a sufficient Stock to go on with; and even that will leffen, if no Pains be taken to increafe it. Continued Application then is a Duty of Importance. Perfons of lower Abilities and Attainments are in Danger, without it, of being ufelefs and defpifed: and they, who fet out with greater Advantages, are bound to endeavour at doing, in Proportion, greater Services to the Church of God. Without Exception therefore, all who are engaged in fo ferious an Employment as ours, if they have any Regard either to their Duty or their Character, muft take care not to be more remarkable for their Diverfions than their Studies; nor indolently to trifle their Time away, inftead of employing it to good Purpofes. And though moft Parts of Learning will be ufeful to us, and all Parts ornamental; yet we muft be fure to remember what we have been folemnly admonifhed of, that no Attention to any Thing elfe, ought ever to draw us away from the Purfuit of fuch Knowledge, as is properly Theological. For to excel in other Things, and be deficient in that, cannot but caft a grievous Reflection; either on us, for not ftudying what we profefs; or on our Profeffion, as having little in

it

it worth studying. Our principal Business therefore must be, to obtain a thorough Acquaintance with the Christian Faith: first the Grounds, then the Doctrines of it. And the previous Qualifications for attempting this are, a due Knowledge of the Rules of right Reasoning, and of the moral and religious Truths which Nature teaches; of the State of the World in its earlier Ages, and in that when Christianity first appeared. These Preparations being made, the great Thing requisite in the next Place is a diligent Search into Holy Scripture. For there it is, that both the authentic System of our Belief, and the chief Evidence for it, are exhibited to our View. Scripture therefore, above all Things, the Infidel endeavours to ridicule; the mistaken Christian, to wrest in Support of his Errors: and if we desire, either to confute them, or to satisfy ourselves; our only Way must be, to understand it well. For which End it is quite necessary, that we make the original Language, at least of the New Testament, familiar to us: and were that of the Old more commonly studied, the Advantages would be very considerable.

In

In order to see clearly, on what Grounds our Belief stands; together with the sacred Volumes themselves, the Writings of such learned Persons, as have proved their Authority, and vindicated their Accounts of Things, must be carefully read; and attentively compared with those Objections against them, which have been revived of late, dressed up with so much Art, and spread abroad with so much Diligence. For in our present Circumstances we are always liable to be attacked: and consider, what an unhappy Triumph it would afford, should we be found unprovided of a rational Defence. It is very true, the general Evidence, which we have for our Faith is abundantly sufficient of itself, to overbalance many Difficulties concerning it, and ever so many Cavils against it. But yet our being unqualified to give more particular Answers, where they can be given; as indeed there are few Cases, where they cannot; may often prove a great Reproach to Us, and a great Stumbling-block to others.

Next to the Grounds of Religion, the Doctrines of it, especially the more important and disputed ones, ought to be studied, with such Diligence

Diligence and Impartiality, as may beſt diſcover to us the Nature of every Opinion, and the Force of every Argument: that ſo we may neither load Chriſtianity with what doth not belong to it; nor betray, inſtead of defending it, by giving up what doth; but faithfully *keep that which is committed to our Truſt*[c], both entire and unmixed. To ſecure this great End, we muſt ever adhere ſtrictly to the Word of God, fairly interpreted by the Help of all ſuch Means as Providence hath given us; and carefully avoid, on the one Hand, Fondneſs of Novelty; and, on the other, over-great Reverence of Antiquity, eſpecially ſuch as comes ſhort of the earlieſt. But againſt the former of theſe, it is peculiarly needful to caution the riſing Generation; whom the Raſhneſs of Youth, and the petulant Spirit of the preſent Age, too often hurries into a ſtrange Vehemence for any Imagination, which they have happened to take up: and prompts them to fly out againſt eſtabliſhed Doctrines, without having always the Patience even to underſtand them. Such therefore ſhould be exhorted to learn a pro-

[c] 1 Tim. vi. 20.

per Degree, both of Silence and Sufpence, till cooler Thought, and farther Inquiry, make them fitter Judges of Things. But befides thofe Controverfies, to which this Caution chiefly relates; that between the Papifts and Us deferves at prefent to be well ftudied, by fuch of you, as live in the Neighbourhood of any. For feldom have they fhewn more Zeal or more Artifice, than of late, in their Attempts of making Profelytes. And therefore it is of great Confequence, that we provide ourfelves againft them, with a fufficient Knowledge of their real Doctrines, their moft fpecious Pleas, and the proper Anfwers to them. Another Subject, with which we are concerned to be well acquainted, is what relates to the Government and Worfhip Difcipline and Eftablifhment of our own Church. Different Parts of our Ecclefiaftical Conftitution are frequently cenfured, by different Sorts of Perfons, with very different Views: though indeed the moft oppofite of them have appeared, for fome Time, unaccountably difpofed to unite againft us; and Believers to join with Infidels in ufing their Chriftian Brethren ill. It may therefore be of great Use, to inform ourselves diligently concerning every Thing of this Nature, which is spoken of to our Prejudice; and be always ready to shew the genuine State of the Case, with Mildness and Fairness. But no Controversies, however needful, must be suffered to divert our Attention from what is of all Things the most needful, the Study of practical Religion, and of the common Duties of Life. These are the Things, which Mankind are most apt to fail in, and most concerned not to fail in: and therefore spending much Time upon them, obtaining a thorough Insight into them, and having a deep Sense of them, is the very Foundation of doing good both to others and to our own Souls.

A competent Provision of Knowledge being supposed, the next Thing is communicating it to those who are under our Care, in such Manner as their Circumstances require.

The Proofs of Religion, both natural and revealed, all Men should be taught, and especially at present, in the most intelligible and convincing Manner. As for the Objections against either: such as it may be supposed they have thought or heard of, should be distinctly

distinctly answered; but the rest obviated only as Occasion offers. For to enter into them farther, would be mispending Time. Next to the Truth of Religion, they should have its Importance laid before them. The Necessity of a moral Life most Men will own in general Terms: only what they are pleased to call so, is often a very immoral one, both with Respect to their Fellow-Creatures and the Government of themselves. But Regard to Piety is strangely lost, even amongst Persons, that are otherwise tolerably serious. Many have laid aside all Appearances of it: and others, who would seem to keep them up, do it with evident Marks of Indifference and Contempt. It should therefore be industriously shewn and inculcated, that an inward Sense of Love and Duty to God, founded on just Conceptions of him, and expressing itself in frequent Acts of Worship, constant Obedience and Resignation to him, is in Truth *the first and great Commandment*[d], the principal and most important of moral Obligations. But then, besides those Instances of Piety, which Reason requires of

[d] Matt. xxii. 38.

us, there are others, founded on Relations equally real, and consequently deserving equal Regard, enjoined by Revelation. The utmost Care therefore ought to be used, considering the present Disposition of the World, to convince Men of what Moment the Doctrines and Duties of the Gospel are. To make Reason sufficient for Nothing in Religion is, to overturn every Thing. But to insist on its Insufficiency for many most valuable Purposes, which Revelation is fully sufficient for, and on the Necessity of observing whatever God hath thought fit to command, this is doing but common Justice, though a very seasonable Piece of Justice, to the Doctrine of our Blessed Saviour, and the Authority of our Maker.

When once Men are brought to understand the Value of Christianity, the next Thing is, to give them a proportionable Solicitude for it: to make them observe, how visibly the Belief and Practice of it decay, and how dreadful the Consequences must be, and are: to shew them, that Religion is not the Concern of the Clergy merely, but the common Concern of All Men; the great Thing, on which public and private Happiness depends in this Life, as well

well as eternal Felicity in the next: that therefore, if they have any Value for these important Interests, they must take the necessary Means of securing them: their Children, their Servants and Dependants must be diligently watched over and instructed; private Devotion must be practised, Family-Worship revived, and the Service of God in the Church regularly and seriously attended upon. For laying aside these Things hath almost banished Religion from amongst us: and Nothing, but restoring them, can bring it back. Piety is indeed seated in the Heart: but to give it no Vent in outward Expression, is to stifle and extinguish it. Neglecting the public Exercise of Religion, is destroying the public Regard to it: and teaching Men to despise their own Form of Religion, is enough very often to make them despise it under any Form.

Great Pains have been taken by our Adversaries to give the World an ill Opinion of religious Instruction: and we must take equal Pains to give them a good one of it; by representing to them, both the natural Influence it hath, and the divine Authority that enjoins it,

it. But after all, the only effectual Conviction will be that of Experience. And therefore the chief Point is, endeavour that Men may feel the Benefit of our teaching: feel at least, that it is their own Fault, not ours, if they do not become the wiser, the better and happier for it. To this End, we must all dwell often and strongly on the great Duties, and great Failures of Duty in common Life: first explaining the Obligations of Religion so as that they may be practised; then insisting on it, that they must: entering into the Particulars of each with such Plainness, that every one may clearly see his own Faults laid before him; yet with such Prudence, that no one may so much as imagine himself personally pointed at: and taking the strictest Care, that no Part of what we say may seem in the least to proceed from our own Passions, or our own Interests; but all appear evidently to flow from a true Concern for the Good of those that hear us. Diligent Consideration, what our Subject and our several Characters will bear us out in, must direct us, when to give our Judgment with Diffidence, when to lay Stress upon it:

in

in what Cases to *exhort with all Long-suffering*[e]; in what, to *rebuke with all Authority*[f]. But whichsoever we do, neither our Language should be florid, nor our Manner theatrical: for these Things only raise an useless Admiration in weak Persons, and produce great Contempt in judicious ones. Nor yet on the other Hand, should our Expressions be mean, or our Behaviour lifeless: but both must be suitable to the Employment we are upon; both be such as come naturally from the Heart of the Speaker, and therefore will naturally move that of the Hearer.

To this our public Teaching it will be a great Help, and indeed a valuable Part of it, if we perform the several Offices of our excellent Liturgy devoutly and properly: neither with an irreverent Precipitation, nor a tedious Slowness: neither in a flat and languid Manner, nor yet with an affected Liveliness, or a Vehemence ill-placed or over-done: but so as may best express the Sense and the Importance of what we read; and, by shewing our own Attention to it, engage that of all around us.

[e] 2 Tim. iv. 2.   [f] Tit. ii. 15.

Besides

Besides our general Instructions, it is very needful, that we give the Youth under our Care, in particular, an early Knowledge and Love of Religion, that may abide with them: and stand the Trials, to which their riper Years will of Course be exposed. I hope you are all diligent in that most useful Work of Catechizing; and have done your utmost to prepare for Confirmation, those whom you present to me. And I earnestly recommend it to you, that the good Impressions, which may well be supposed to have been made upon their Minds at this Season, be not suffered to wear off again; but be improved into settled Habits of Religion and Virtue, by still farther Exhortations, and leading them, as soon as possible, to the Holy Communion. But though all the Youth deserve our peculiar Attention; yet if any of them be educated in Charity-Schools under our Inspection, for these we should think ourselves still more nearly concerned, than for the rest; and, by first taking Care, to have them taught whatever is proper, and Nothing else, then making known the good Management they are under, put an End to those Accusations, of their

learning

learning Idleness and Pride, Superstition and Disloyalty; which may have been, sometimes one of them, sometimes another, in some Degree deserved; but have been carried with a wicked Industry most shamefully beyond Truth, and lessened the Credit of this excellent Institution, even with many good Persons, to the great Detriment of Christianity.

Another very useful Method of spreading the Knowledge of Religion, and teaching Men a serious Regard to it, is by distributing, or procuring to be distributed, such pious Books, especially to the poorer Sort, as are best suited to their Capacities and Circumstances. For there is great Variety of them to be had: and at so very low Prices, that much Good may be done this Way to considerable Numbers at once, in a most acceptable Manner, for a trifling Expence.

But Nothing will contribute more to make our public Instructions effectual, than private Conversation, directed with prudence to the same End. The better we are known to Persons, the greater Influence we may hope to have upon them: and the better we know them,

them, the more diftinctly we fhall fee how to make Ufe of that Influence to good Purpofes. By reprefenting proper Truths, at fit Times, with a modeft Freedom, we may very much abate the Prejudices of Men, who have any Fairnefs remaining, both againft Religion and ourfelves: at leaft we may prevail on them, for the Sake of public Order, and Example, to keep within the Bounds of Decency; and fo prevent their doing Harm, if we cannot make them Good. Perfons, that err in particular Points of Doctrine, friendly Difcourfe may fhew us what led them into their Miftakes, and enable us to lead them out again. Such as diffent from our Church Government and Worfhip, talking amicably with them, and behaving in the fame Manner towards them, if it doth not immediately bring them over, may however bring them nearer to us, both in Judgment and Affection. Such as are faulty in their moral Conduct, ferious and affectionate Remonftrances, given in private and kept private, and joined with a Tendernefs to their Characters in public, may often do a great deal towards reforming them; and fooner or later, the Seed thus fown may fpring up in their

Hearts,

Hearts, and produce happy Fruits. We should not indeed press upon persons, when there is no other Prospect than that of provoking them: but we ought to watch all Opportunities, whilst there is any Hope left; and not only make it our Endeavour to convert the Mistaken and Vicious, but stir up the Negligent to serious Thought, and the Good themselves to more eminent Goodness. Especially such Persons of Rank and influence, as we find well disposed, these we must earnestly excite to appear and give Countenance to the Cause of Religion, ever remembering that awful Declaration of our Blessed Lord: *Whosoever shall be ashamed of me and of my Words in this adulterous and sinful Generation, of him also shall the Son of Man be ashamed, when he cometh in the Glory of his Father, with the holy Angels* [s]. We must convince them of the urgent Necessity there is, for interposing in Behalf of Piety and Virtue: and suggest to them the Means for engaging with Success in this excellent Employment. Yet must we never spend so much of our Attention on the higher Part of the World, as

[s] Mark viii. 38.

to give the least Suspicion of neglecting the lower; whose Number is so much larger, whose Dispositions are usually so much more favourable to Religion, and whose eternal Happiness is of equal Importance to Them, and ought to be of equal Concern to Us: but we must prove we are in earnest in our Work, by making it our Care, as it was our Master's, that *the Poor have the Gospel preached to them*[h]. And one Opportunity of preaching it with singular Advantage, both to the Poor and the Rich, is when Sickness brings them the View of another Life. At some near to Times indeed the Sick may be incapable of attending to Exhortations: at others they may be endangered by them: and at all Times great Prudence is requisite, to avoid the Extremes, of terrifying or indulging them too much. But, provided due Caution be used in these Respects; laying before them what they ought to be, and reminding them to consult their own Consciences what they have been, is a most likely Method of exciting in them such Affections and Resolutions at that Season of

[h] Matt. xi. 5.

Recollection

Recollection and Seriousness, as, though the Blessing of Heaven, may produce the happiest Effects.

To these excellent Offices therefore we must all of us chearfully apply ourselves, each in such Degree as his Station requires. If they do require Pains, if they do take up Time, if they are inconsistent with agreeable Amusements, and even interrupt useful Studies of other Kinds; yet this is the Business which we have solemnly chosen, and the Vows of God are upon us: it is the most important and most honourable, it ought to be the most delightful too of all Employments: and therefore we have every Reason not to seek the Means of evading our Duty, but of fulfilling it; and each to *take the Oversight of the Flock of God*, committed to him, *not by constraint, but willingly*[i]. For if we only just do what we can be punished by our Superiors for neglecting, we must neither expect Success nor Reward.

But then to secure either, the chief Thing requisite, is still behind: that our own Tempers and Lives be such, as we say those of other Persons should. For if we, who teach

[i] Pet. v. 2.

Religion,

Religion, live, or suffer our Families to live, with little or no Sense of Religion, what can we possibly expect, but that Men will improve so palpable an Advantage against us to the utmost: will argue, that we believe not our own Doctrine; and therefore it deserves no Belief: or, we practise not our own Precepts; and therefore they cannot be practised? Thus we shall increase that infidelity and Wickedness, which our business is to oppose. Too much of it will be really owing to us: and the Whole will be laid upon us. The Enemies of Religion will have the best Pretence in the World to ruin us: and the Friends of it will grow unconcerned for us, and ready to give us up to them. But, were these Consequences not to follow, still very bad ones must follow. Men, irreligious or vicious themselves, cannot be hearty in opposing Irreligion and Vice: they cannot do it with Boldness, if they were hearty: and could they be ever so bold, it must fit much too ill upon them, to have any good Effect. Wrong-minded Persons will be furnished with the most plausible Excuse imaginable for disregarding them intirely: and the rightest-minded Persons that ever were, cannot, if

they

they would, regard them as they ought. This will be the Case, even with Respect to their public Teaching: and as for private Admonitions, they will seldom have the Face to venture upon them, and never succeed in them: whereas every Word, that comes from an exemplary Man, hath great Weight; and his bare Example is most valuable Instruction of itself. But, were a bad Life not to hinder at all the Success of our Ministry; yet we must remember, it will absolutely hinder the Salvation of our Souls: and subject us to that *sorer Punishment, of which he may well be thought worthy, who, teaching others, teacheth not himself, but through breaking the Law dishonoureth God*[k].

Nor is it sufficient by any Means for us to be guilty of no Vice. This is small Praise, for one of our Order. We are bound to be Patterns of the most diligent Practice of Virtue, and the strictest Regard to Religion: and we shall never make others zealous for what we ourselves appear indifferent about. It is very true, that peculiarly in our Case, the Generality of the World both expect and find

[k] Heb. x. 29.   Rom. ii. 21, 23.

Fault, quite beyond Reason: and doubtless they are much to blame in doing so. But then surely we are no less to blame, if, when we know the Severity, with which our Conduct will be examined, we do not watch over it with equal Severity ourselves; and take the only Way to be looked on as good Men, that is, being such undeniably. And whoever hath a due Sense of this Obligation, will conscientiously *abstain*, not only *from all Evil*, but, *all Appearance* of it too[l]. Such a one, for Instance, far from ever offending against Temperance, will be noted for it: and think the Imputation of being *mighty to drink Wine*[m] almost as infamous, as that of being overcome by it. Far from being guilty of Indecency in his Behaviour or Discourse, he will keep at a Distance from every Thing liable to the Construction of it. Far from being remarkable for Luxury and Delicacy in his Manner of living or appearing, he will be sure to preserve himself, on all Occasions, at least as remote from Indulgence, as he is from Austerity. And though he will never disgust the Persons,

[l] 1 Thess. v. 22.   [m] Is. v. 22.

with

with whom he converses, by a Gravity affected or ill timed: yet he will be equally careful, never to expose himself, by a Lightness of Carriage unbecoming his Function; nor let any Thing be a Part of his Character, much less a distinguishing Part, that can only tend to lower it. For we can never be useful, if we are despised: and we shall be despised, if we will give Opportunities for it. Even they who seem well pleased with us will think meanly of us inwardly; and perhaps of the whole Order for our Sakes.

Yet at the same Time, we shall be greatly mistaken, if we aim to avoid Contempt by Haughtiness: which will only add Hatred to it. Our Rule therefore must be, to express, in every Thing, Condescension to the lower Part of the World, without being improperly familiar; and Respect to the upper, without being servile: recommending ourselves at once to the Love and Esteem of both by a mild Kind of Dignity and ingenuous Simplicity, kept up through our whole Behaviour. Mildness of Temper is the Duty of every Man; but especially required

required of Us [n]; and abfolutely neceffary, both to our preferving Regard, and doing Service in the World. Therefore, whatever Provocations we meet with from thofe, amongft whom we live, as indeed we often meet with great ones, it neither belongs to our Character, nor will be for our Intereft, to take Offence and exprefs Refenment; but by Prudence and Patience to *overcome Evil with good* [o]. For we fhall often do it this Way, and never any other. Inftead of being engaged in Enmities of our own, it fhould be our Endeavour to compofe the Differences of other Perfons: not by intermeddling in their Affairs, when we are not called to it; but by laying hold on every fit Opportunity given us, for difpofing them to a mutual good Opinion, where there is Room for it; or at leaft to mutual Good-will. Too many Occafions indeed for friendly Interpofition, our unhappy Party-Difputes furnifh us with, had we no other. Entering into thefe with Vehemence, and that Injuftice which never fails to accompany Vehemence,

[n] Matt. x. 16. [1] Tim. iii. 3. [2] Tim. ii. 24. [o] Rom. xii. 21.

is what all Men should avoid: but we, who must caution them against it, should avoid it with uncommon Care: should religiously pay that Respect to every one, which is their Due, especially to our Superiors; think well of Mens Actions and Designs, unless we have evident Cause to think otherwise; judge with Modesty, where perhaps we are not qualified to judge; and whatever our Opinion be, preserve our Behaviour inoffensive: give the least Provocation, that may be, to bad Men of any Side; and act in such Manner, as may gain us, if possible, the united Esteem of good Men of all Sides. For theirs is the Friendship, of which we ought to be ambitious. Familiarities with profane and vicious Persons, beyond what necessary Civility, or a real Prospect of reforming them requires, will, whatever we may promise ourselves from their Favour or Interest, always discredit and weaken us in general; and much oftener prove hurtful, than advantageous, to any of us in particular. But to cultivate the good Opinion of the wise and virtuous, to recommend ourselves to their Protection, and, whatever else they may differ about, engage their common Zeal in the common Cause of Religion; this will procure us both Security and Honour, and every Way promote the great Design of our Profession.

Another Point, on which our Character will not a little depend, is our being, in a reasonable Degree, disinterested. A very large Proportion indeed of the Clergy have too much Cause to endeavour at bettering their Circumstances: and it is barbarous Treatment, to accuse them for it, instead of pitying them. But over-great Solicitude and Contrivance for advancing ourselves will always make Impressions to our Prejudice, let our Condition be ever so low: though deservedly much stronger Impressions, in Proportion as it is higher. We shall be thought to have no Attention, but that, of which we discover too much: and the Truth is, *we cannot serve two Masters*[p]. Nor will it be sufficient, that we avoid the Charge of immoderately desiring more; unless we avoid also that of Selfishness, in the Management of what we have already: a Matter, in which

[p] Matth. vi. 24.

it is very difficult, and yet very important, to give no offence. We are bound, both to thofe who belong to us, and thofe who fhall come after us, to take a proper Care of our legal Dues: and preferve them faithfully from the Encroachments of fuch, as tell us very truly, that we ought not to be worldly-minded; but forget, what is equally true, that they themfelves ought not to be fo. But then the ftrongeft Reafons of all Kinds oblige us, never to make unjuft or litigious Claims; never to do any Thing, either hard and rigorous, or mean and fordid: to fhew, that we defire always the moft eafy and amicable Method of ending Difputes; and whatever Method we may be forced to take, never to let any Thing force us into the leaft Degree of Unfairnefs, Paffion or Ill-will; but endeavour, by all Inftances of friendly Behaviour, to win, if poffible, upon the Perfon we have to do with; at leaft to convince every Body elfe, how very far we are from intending Wrong to Him, or any one.

And Nothing will contribute more, to acquit us from the Sufpicion of being felfifh in our Dealings with other Perfons; than approving ourselves charitable to the Poor: a Virtue which becomes us so extremely, and is so peculiarly expected from us, and will give us so valuable an Influence; that we should willingly straighten ourselves in almost any Thing besides, that to the full Proportion of our Abilities, we may abound in giving Alms. And together with this, would we but, each in his Station, take the best Care we can to see Justice done them in that Provision, which the Law hath intended for them, it would generally prove a much more considerable Benefaction, than all that we are able to bestow on them of our own.

To the above-mentioned Instances of right Conduct we must always add, what will render them very engaging, the occasional kind Offices of good Neighbourhood; with a decent Hospitality also, if our Circumstances will permit it: and then, notwithstanding the Censures of those, who complain that we are of little Use, and endeavour to make us of none; we may surely well hope to do Service to God, and be esteemed of Men: especially if, together with so exemplary a Behaviour

towards

towards others, we are friendly and compassionate, candid and equitable amongst ourselves.

Great Injustice, I am satisfied, is done us on this Head: and many groundless Accusations brought confidently against us, by Persons, who neither enquire into Facts, nor consider Circumstances. But there are few Things, in which it concerns us more, to clear ourselves where we are innocent, and to amend ourselves where we are faulty. For so long as we are thought in the World, either insolent to our inferior Brethren in general, or void of Generosity and Pity to such of them as we employ; we must not expect to receive better Treatment, than we are understood to give. And if we are believed to be chargeable, beyond other Men, with mutual Bitterness and Vehemence, when any Kind of Controversy rises amongst us; this too is a Character, so very different from that which ought to be ours, that the utmost Care should be taken to guard against it. Not that we are obliged, either to speak of or behave to men of bad Lives, or bad Principles, as if they were good ones, because

cause unhappily they belong to our Order. Making no Distinction would be on all Accounts wrong: and making a proper Distinction will be very useful. But then we should never think worse of our Brethren, than Evidence forces us; never publish our ill Opinion, without sufficient Reason; nor exceed, when we do publish it, the Bounds of Moderation: we should be ready to shew them all fitting Kindness, even whilst they continue blameable; and receive them back with the most charitable Tenderness, when they return to their Duty. For there is no Manner of Need, that we should give either so much Advantage or so much Pleasure to the Adversaries of Religion, as to let them see those, who should be the Joint-defenders of it, engaged in domestic Wars: and bringing such Charges, and raising such Prejudices, one against another, that it is hard to say, whether believing or disbelieving our mutual Accusations will make the World think worse of us. Our blessed Lord therefore, after reminding his Disciples, that *they were the Salt of the Earth*; were designed, by the Purity of their Doctrine and Example,

ample, to keep others from Corruption; and after giving them that prophetic Warning, that we shall find Men zealous to fulfil, that *if the Salt have lost its Savour, it shall be cast out and trodden under Foot* [q]; resuming the same Figure at another Time, concludes his Exhortation thus, *Have Salt in yourselves; and have Peace one with another* [r].

To these Things, Brethren, if we have any Concern for the Interests of Religion or our own, we must always industriously attend; but especially in such Times, as by no Means admit of Negligence or Mismanagement. Yet vain will our best Endeavours be, unless we constantly add to them our fervent Prayers, that God would enable and strengthen, both Us, and all that serve him in the Gospel of his Son, to perform our Duty with Faithfulness and Success. For *we are not sufficient to think any Thing of ourselves: our Sufficiency is of God* [s]. What therefore we ought, every one of us, to beg of him at all Times, let us all at present jointly address to

[q] Matth. v. 13.   [r] Mark ix. 50.   [s] 2 Cor. iii. 5.

him

him for, in the comprehensive and expressive Words of our public Service.

Almighty and everlasting God, by whose Spirit the whole Body of the Church is governed and sanctified; receive our Supplications and Prayers, which we offer before thee for all Estates of Men in thy holy Church; that every Member of the same, in his Vocation and Ministry, may truly and godly serve thee, through our Lord and Saviour Jesus Christ. Amen[t].

[t] Second Collect for *Good Friday*.

A CHARGE

DELIVERED TO THE

CLERGY of the DIOCESE

OF

OXFORD,

In the YEAR 1741.

Reverend Brethren,

WHEN I had first the Pleasure of meeting you, being very much a Stranger, I could only lay before you such general Admonitions as appeared to be seasonable in this unhappy Age of Irreligion and Libertinism. But having now obtained a fuller Acquaintance with Things, chiefly from your Answers to my printed Enquiries, which have given me many Reasons to esteem and respect you; I shall at present descend into some farther Particulars: and considering you, not merely as Ministers of the Gospel at large, but as Ministers of the several Parishes in which you officiate, remind you of some plain Directions for your doing it more successfully: which I shall deliver with less Diffidence, and you will receive with greater Regard, for their being chiefly such as have been often recommended

mended with good Effect on such Occasions as this.

I begin with one of the lowest in Appearance, but not the least important of ecclesiastical Employments: Catechizing the Children under your Care.

The Catechism consists of the fundamental Articles of Christian Faith and Practice. Without learning these we know not so much as what it is we profess to be; and there is great Danger that unless Persons learn them at first, they will never learn them thoroughly: but only pick up from what they hear or read, unconnected and sometimes ill grounded Notions, that will never unite into a complete or a consistent Form of sound Doctrine: as I apprehend we have had too much Experience. The Rubric therefore requires, *that every Person learn the Catechism before his Confirmation:* and the 59th Canon, that *every Incumbent shall examine and instruct the young and ignorant of his Parish in it for half an Hour or more every Sunday.* Every second Sunday had been appointed before: but that I suppose was judged afterwards insufficient. Not that a strict Observation of this Rule was

probably

probably expected, during the Winter Season, in the Generality of Country Parishes, or where the Children being few, were more easily taught. But plainly it was intended, that how much Time soever was needful to do this Work well, should be faithfully employed in it. I thank God, there are very few Places in this Diocese, and I hope there will soon be none, where Catechising is omitted. But I observe that in many it is practised only during Lent. Now I should apprehend that the Summer Season would in general be much more convenient both for the Minister and the Congregation. But at least the Space of a few Weeks is by no means sufficient to fix the Knowledge of their Christian Duty so firmly in the Minds of young People, but that in the many Months which pass from the End of one Lent to the Beginning of another, a great Part of it will be to learn again. Therefore whenever this Exercise is begun, it should be continued much longer: and whenever the constant Repetition of it is left off, it should be occasionally resumed for a Sunday or two, at proper Distances of Time.

Another Defect in some Places is, that barely the Words of the Catechism are taught without any Exposition. Now the very plainest Expressions in it will need to be varied into others that are equivalent: else Children will too often learn nothing but the Sound: and unless this Danger, which is a very great one, be guarded against, you will have spent both their Pains and your own to but small Purpose. Besides, all Sciences have their Terms, which must be interpreted to Beginners: and some of those in the Catechism are figurative ones; very prudently used, as they comprehend in a little Compass much Meaning, and lead to the understanding of the same Figures in Scripture; but undoubtedly used on Purpose to be explained: without which they are liable to make either no Impression, or a wrong one. And farther still, a System so short as to be learned by Heart, must have Need, were it ever so clear, to be enlarged on; the Proofs of its Truth, the Connections and Tendency of its Doctrines, the Use and Extent of its Precepts to be shewn: and therefore since the Canon

non with great Reason enjoins, not only that you examine, but instruct the Children in their Catechism, I hope you will think this a very needful Part of that Instruction. As to the Manner of it, that may be different, not only in different Places, but in the same at different Times. Sometimes a continued Discourse of some Length may be requisite: as it will lay before the adult Part of your Parishioners a methodical Summary of Christian Doctrine; which they often want very much for themselves, and will thus be enabled to teach something of to their Children, after they have heard it together from you.

Sometimes a cursory Exposition of the more difficult Expressions may deserve the Preference. But asking the Children Questions, relating to each Part, and procuring them to learn Texts of Scripture confirming each, will be always beneficial. The Words of the Catechism itself may be very usefully broken into shorter Questions and Answers: to which others may be added out of any one of the many good Expositions that have been made public. Only you should endeavour as soon and as much as you can to make this

a Trial

a Trial and Improvement of the Understanding, as well as the Memory of young People, by asking such Things as they should reply to in Words of their own; making that easy to them in every possible Way. And indeed, if many of your Questions were formed to be answered merely by affirming or denying, it would be a very good Method; and there is an Exposition drawn up in that Manner.

I am sensible that some Clergymen are unhappily obliged to serve two Churches the same Afternoon: who may therefore plead, that they have scarce ever Time to hear the Children repeat their Catechism, much less to explain it to them. And God forbid that any needless Addition should ever be made to their Burthen. But as I am sure they will be desirous of doing what they are able, in a Matter of this Importance, so I should hope that in the longer Days, at each of their Churches alternately, they might hear the Catechism repeated one Sunday, and expound Part of another, or hear only Part of it repeated, and expound that, or find some Way to prevent the intire Omission of so necessary a Duty. And if these can do any Thing of this

Kind,

Kind, there is no Doubt but others may easily do more.

But a farther Hindrance which I fear you complain of too justly is, that Parents and Masters are negligent in sending their Children and Servants; and the latter especially are both unwilling and often ashamed to come. Now the Canon doth indeed make Provision for punishing such. But persuading them would be much happier. And surely in so clear a Case, well timed and well judged Arguments, if persisted in, must do a great deal. The Example of their Equals or their Betters, if you have any under your Care that are wise enough to set a good one; or however that of your own Families, may help very much: and such little Rewards of good Books, or other Encouragements as you can give or procure for them, it may be hoped, will completely prevail with them. At least such as think they are either too old or too considerable to say the Catechism themselves, may be greatly improved by hearing others repeat, and you explain it.

But in some few Places it is pleaded, that the Children cannot read, and their Parents either

either cannot or will not get them taught, and therefore the Foundation for their learning the Catechism is wanting. But surely some Person might be found, within a moderate Distance from every Place, to whom Parents might be induced, at least if something were contributed towards it, to send their Children to be instructed thus far. Or at the worst, they who cannot read might easily by Degrees learn so much as the Catechism by Heart: especially as the three main Parts of it are in every Sunday's Prayers. The Incapacity of reading was almost general at the Time of the Reformation: yet even in those Days the Clergy were able to teach first Parents and Housholders, then by their Means Children and Servants, the Lord's Prayer, the Creed, and the Ten Commandments: and afterwards the rest of the Catechism. Now since that gross Darkness hath been so far enlightened, it cannot be impracticable to dispel the Remains of it.

After due Instruction follows Confirmation: an Appointment derived down from Apostolical Practice; and of such acknowledged Usefulness, that in the Times of Confusion, a
hundred

hundred Years ago, when Bishops were rejected, some of their Adversaries took upon them to perform this Part of their Function: and within these few Years the Church of *Geneva* hath restored it in the best Manner their Form of Church Government will admit, and added an Office for it to their Liturgy. In our own Church the ancient Esteem of this Institution is, generally speaking, so well preserved, that I hope the Desire of being confirmed may not a little strengthen that of being instructed, as the only Way to it. And yet I must observe, that the Numbers from some Parishes have been in Proportion very small. This may not have arisen from any Neglect in the Minister: but as it ought to incline me to make the Opportunities of Confirmation as convenient as I am able; so it ought to incline you, agreeably to the Nature of your Function, and the express Direction of the 61st Canon, to use your best Endeavours, that your Parishioners may gladly take those Opportunities. Yet I must entreat you to endeavour at the same Time, that none be brought, but those who, to speak in the Language of the Rubric, *are come to Years of Discretion*, who have learned, not the Words only, but in a competent Degree, the Meaning of what was promised for them in Baptism; who can say with Seriousness and Truth, (what surely else they ought not to say at all,) that *in the Presence of God and the Congregation they ratify and confirm the same in their own Persons*; and who therefore are likely to have useful and lasting Impressions made on them by this Solemnity. Undoubtedly some arrive at this Capacity sooner than others, and therefore I have mentioned the Age of Fourteen, not with a Design of absolutely tying you down to it; but as being, for the most part, full early enough; and that, where you see it requisite, you may, without giving Offence yourselves, oppose my Order to the indiscreet Forwardness of Parents; whom however, I hope, it will make easy, to assure them, as I give you Authority, that so long as it pleases God to continue my Health and Strength, Confirmations shall be frequent in every Part of this Diocese. I must also desire that you will carefully instruct those whom you do bring, in the whole Nature of the Institution and particularly in this, amongst other

other more important Points, that they are never to be confirmed any more than baptized a second Time: that you will direct them to make the proper Answers audibly through the Whole of the Office, which many of them seem to have no Notion of, though it is so necessary in the Nature of the Thing, and tends so much both to fix their Attention, and to give the Solemnity a decent and edifying Appearance. You will caution them likewise not to crowd forward and incommode each other, using this Argument for one, that the whole Number who come in at the same Time, will be dismissed at the same Time also: and lastly you will press it strongly upon their Minds, that what they promise at their Confirmation, they are to remember and keep to their Lives End. I have already desired of you, on these Occasions, a List of such as you judge qualified; that so the Numbers and Persons may be known: of this you would do well to keep a Copy yourselves, and if it were written alphabetically, both you and I should be able to consult it upon the Spot more easily. For the abovementioned Canon, the 61st, plainly directs your Attendance

ance along with your Parishioners; to take especial Care (for so the Words run) *that none be presented but such as you know are fit.* And as your being present to approve or disapprove must needs increase your Influence and Authority amongst your People; it must likewise make the Discharge of my Duty so very much easier and more useful, that I beg you will never let me be without your Assistance in this Work, as you shall never be without mine in any Thing. And for this Purpose when Confirmations are on a Sunday, which is the Time I shall usually pitch upon, for the Convenience of the People, excepting at the Places of my Visitation, you may omit for that Day the Morning or the Evening Prayers as you see Occasion. I have not indeed hitherto been able to effect, what would greatly shorten your Labour, calling up your several Parishes in their Order separately. But I shall be very glad to do it, as soon as ever you can introduce this Order amongst them, which I earnestly recommend to you: and I hope a continued Frequency of Confirmations will soon make that feasible without Difficulty here, which is now practised practifed conftantly in the populous Cities of *London* and *Weftminfter*.

From Confirmation Perfons ought to be led on, if poffible, before the Impreffions of it are much weakened, to the holy Sacrament: and it is one material Reafon why Confirmation fhould not be too early, that with a little farther Inftruction given foon after it, you may eafily bring them, fuch as they ought to be, to the Lord's Table: which may prove a much harder Matter, when once they have been a good While out of your Hands. The fmall Proportion of Communicants which I find there is in moft of your Congregations, and very fmall in fome, muft undoubtedly (as this Ordinance is appointed for all Chriftians, and for a ftanding Means of Grace to all) be a Subject of very great Concern to you. And though it is too true, that the Generality of the World, and perhaps the lower Sort beyond others, are incredibly obftinate in their Prejudices, especially in fuch as at all favour corrupt Nature: yet our complaining of thefe Prejudices is not enough; but labouring to overcome them is our Bufinefs, and we are not to grow weary

of

of it. Some imagine that the Sacrament belongs only to Persons of advanced Years, or great Leisure, or high Attainments in Religion, and is a very dangerous Thing for common Persons to venture upon. Some again disregard it stupidly, because others, they say, who do receive, are never the better for it; or because their Friends before them, or their Neighbours about them never received at all, or not till such an Age: and why should they? You will therefore represent to them, that whoever receives without Benefit, it is his own Fault; and that how many soever omit it either for Part of their Lives or the Whole, not their Example but the Word of God, is the Rule for Christians: that far from being a terrible or ensnaring Institution, it is in Reality a most gracious one: designed to be celebrated with Humility indeed, but with Comfort and Joy: that all the Preparation it requires is within the Reach of the plainest Head and the most laborious Hand, provided there be only an honest and pious Heart: and that the Judgment which unworthy Receivers eat and drink to themselves, needs no more af-

fright

fright those whom God in his Mercy will consider as worthy; as he certainly will every true Penitent; than the capital Punishments, threatened by the Law to Crimes, make innocent Persons uneasy: that he whose Life unfits him for the Sacrament, is unfit for the Kingdom of Heaven also; and he, who being qualified for it, neglects it, neglects a dying Command of his Lord and Saviour, intended for the greatest Good to him. But your public Instructions on this Head will be much more effectual for being followed by seasonable private Applications: in which you will hear and answer their Objections, be they of ever so little Weight, with great Meekness; not be provoked by any Perverseness of theirs to shew Anger, but only a friendly Concern; and even if you meet with an absolute Repulse, leave them with an Assurance that you shall apply to them again, in Hopes that God will have disposed them better to obey his Precepts.

But besides increasing the Number of your Communicants, it were very desirable, that they who do communicate should do it more frequently. In the three first Centuries the Eucharist

Eucharist was every where celebrated weekly, and in many Places almost daily. Decay of Piety occasioned an Injunction in the Sixth, that every Christian should receive thrice in the Year; which was reduced in the Thirteenth, perhaps with a bad Intention, to once. Our Church requires thrice *at the least*: which evidently implies, that more than thrice is hoped for. And indeed each Person will scarce be able to communicate so often unless the Communion be administered oftener. But besides, it is appointed to be every Lord's Day in Cathedral and Collegiate Churches, and Part of the Office for it is read every Lord's Day in every Church, for an Admonition of what it were to be wished the People could be brought to. This indeed at best must be a Work of Time; but one Thing might be done at present in all your Parishes, as God be thanked, it is in most of them: a Sacrament might easily be interposed in that long Interval between *Whitsuntide* and *Christmas*: and the usual Season for it, about the Feast of *St. Michael*, (when your People having gathered in the Fruits of the Earth have some

some Rest from their Labours, and must surely feel some Gratitude to the Giver of all Good) is a very proper Time. And if afterwards you can advance from a quarterly Communion to a monthly one, I make no Doubt but you will.

Upon this Subject I must observe to you farther, that though in one or two Parishes of this Diocese the old Custom is retained, of Oblations for the Minister, as well as Alms for the Poor, to both which the Sentences appointed to be read are plainly adapted: yet in many Parishes there is no Offertory at all: though it be certainly a Practice of primitive Antiquity, a most proper Admonition and Specimen of Charity; which I fear the Generality of Christians much want to be reminded of; a most seasonable Demonstration of our loving our Brethren for his Sake, who hath loved us; and a Thing expresly enjoined in the Rubric of the Communion Office. Why therefore should you not attempt to revive it, where it hath been intermitted? Merely presenting to Persons an Opportunity of giving, if they think fit, and only what they think

think fit, can surely (if the Reasons of it be explained to them beforehand) never keep any one away from the Sacrament. But then, though all who have not absolutely Nothing, ought undoubtedly to contribute their Mite, yet no disagreeable Notice should ever be taken of any, for giving but little or not giving at all; and whatever is collected, should be disposed of, so that all Persons may know it, with the greatest Faithfulness, Prudence, and Impartiality.

Another Part of Divine Worship, concerning which I think it needful to speak, is Psalmody: a Part clearly appointed in Scripture, both expressive and productive of devout Affections, extremely well fitted to diversify long Services, and peculiarly to distinguish the several Parts of our own, which were originally separate. Our ecclesiastical Laws do not indeed require it under any Penalty: because there may not every where be Persons qualified to perform it decently. But wherever there are, the Rubric makes Provision for it, and I recommend to you that it be not omitted. You will always endeavour that your Parish-Clerks

Clerks be Persons of Discretion as well as Skill and Seriousness. But however you will be much surer of no Impropriety happening in this Part of the Worship, if you either direct them every Sunday to suitable Psalms, or assign them a Course of such to go orderly through. And unless the generality of your Parishioners are provided with Books, and able to make use of them; ordering each Line to be read, will both secure a greater Number of Singers, and be very instructive to many who cannot sing. All Persons indeed who are by Nature qualified ought, to learn, and constantly join to glorify him that made them, in Psalms and spiritual Songs. This was the Practice of the early Christians: it was restored very justly at the Reformation: and hath declined of late, within most of our Memories, very unhappily. For the Improvements made by a few in Church-Music, were they real Improvements, will seldom equal the Harmony of a general Chorus; in which any lesser Dissonances are quite lost: and it is something inexpressibly elevating, to hear the *Voice of a great Multitude, as the Voice of*

many Waters and of mighty Thunders, to speak in the Words of Scripture, *making a joyful Noise to the God of their Salvation, and singing his Praises with Understanding.* Persons of a ludicrous Turn may represent every Thing in a wrong Light: but those of any Seriousness, if they will lay aside false Delicacy, and that preposterous Shame of religious Performances, with which the present Age is so fatally tainted, will find themselves very piously affected only by hearing this Melody, much more by bearing a Part in it: and therefore I beg you will encourage all your Parishioners, especially the Youth, to learn Psalmody; and excite them, if there be Need, with some little Reward: for you will thus make the Service of God abundantly more agreeable, and their Attendance on it more constant. But then, where any Knowledge of the old common Tunes remains, you should endeavour principally, that your Learners may perfect themselves in these; that so they may lead and assist the rest of the Congregation, who should always join with them; or if you must admit a Mixture of new and uncommon Tunes, it
should

should be no greater than you find yourselves in Prudence absolutely obliged to. Else the Consequence will be, what I fear many of you have experienced, that either one Part of your People will resent being unjustly silenced, and this by the Introduction of Tunes often not so good as their former ones, and so your Parish will be divided and uneasy: or if they agree to the Change ever so generally, and like it ever so well, yet your select Singers will either be weary in a While of what only Novelty recommended to them, or grow conceited and ungovernable, or die off, or be dispersed, and the Congregation will be left unable to sing in any Manner at all. Where indeed the newer Tunes have quite blotted out the Memory of the old ones, all you can do is, to make Use of what you find in Use, to get some of the easiest of them learnt as generally as you can, and keep to these. And if, in order to instruct your People in either Way of Singing, Meetings to practise out of Church-time be requisite, you will keep a strict Watch over them, that they be managed with all possible Decency, and never continued till Candle-light,

light, if they confist of both Sexes. You will likewise difcountenance, at leaft, all frequent Meetings, between the Singers of different Parifhes, and making Appointments to fing alternately at one anothers Churches: for this wandering from their own, which by Law they ought to keep to, ufually leads them into Excefses and Follies.

I am very fenfible, that fome of the Things which I have been mentioning, are by no Means of equal Importance with others. But Nothing is without its Importance, that relates to divine Worfhip. The mere outward Behaviour of thofe who attend upon it is of fuch Ufe, and good Influence, that I muft defire you will be diligent in teaching them, (but fo as to perfuade, not provoke them) what Reverence belongs to the Houfe of God: particularly how very wrong it is to fit inftead of kneeling when they are or fhould be addrefsing themfelves to their Maker, and to fhew how indecent that Appearance is of Difregard to him, which they would not ufe on any Account to one of their Fellow-creatures a little fuperior to themfelves. If they could only breed up the

younger

younger to a right Behaviour in this Respect, your Congregations would grow regular in Time. But mild Expostulations will surely, in so plain a Case, produce some Effect upon the rest also, which will be much facilitated if you take Care that proper Conveniences for kneeling be provided for them. And if you could convince them also that standing is a more reverent Posture to sing Psalms to God in, as well as to read them, than sitting, you would come so much the nearer to the Apostolical Rule *of doing all Things decently*. For as some of the Psalms contain the noblest Acts of Adoration, surely they ought not to be sung in a Posture unfit to express it. Another Thing, and no small one, which I believe many of your Parishioners often want to be admonished of, is to come before the Service begins. Undoubtedly Allowance is to be made for necessary, especially unforeseen, Business, and some Allowance for not knowing the Time exactly: but I hope you will obviate both these Pleas as far as you can, by consulting their Convenience in the Hour you fix, and then keeping punctually to it. And at the same Time you will remind them, that a due Degree of Zeal in Religion would incline them to be rather a great deal too early at the House of God, than a little too late: that no Part of the Service can be more needful for them, than that which comes first; the Confession of their Sins: that Instruction in their Duty is better learnt from the Psalms and Lessons, which are the Word of God, than from Sermons, which are only our Explanations of it: and that by coming so irregularly, they not only are great Losers themselves, but disturb and offend others.

But it is not sufficient to give you Directions about such as do come to Church, without taking Notice of the great Numbers which I find there are in many, if not most, of your Parishes, that omit coming. Now on these your Preaching indeed can have no immediate Influence. But it may however prevent the Increase of them; and furnish others with Arguments against them; and with the best of Arguments, their Experience of its good Effects. You will therefore questionless do all you can in this Way, without using any Expressions in Relation to their Fault, which

if

if repeated to them, may exasperate them. But your chief Dependence must be on private Application to them, varied suitably to the Occasion of their Neglect. If it arises merely from Ignorance, or Sloth, or Want of Thought, they must be plainly told what they owe to their Maker, and awakened to the Hopes and Fears of a future Life. If it be Desire of Gain or of Pleasure that keeps them away, they must be asked what it will *profit them to gain the whole World and lose their own Souls?* or shewn that to be Lovers *of Pleasure more than of God* will end in Pains eternal. If they defend themselves, by pleading, as some will, that Nothing can be told them at Church but what they are acquainted with already, it will surely not be hard to shew them that they over-rate their Knowledge: that if this were otherwise they may however be reminded of what they did not think of, or excited to what they did not practise: that, were they too perfect to receive any Benefit, it would not be decent for them to tell the World so by their Behaviour: that at least they ought to set others an Example who may be the better for public Instruction: and lastly, that receiving Inftruction is not the Whole of divine Service, but Praying the chief Part. And though it is allowed they can pray at Home privately, yet without enquiring whether they do, fince God hath commanded, for plain and important Reafons, that we worfhip him publicly, and hath excepted no one: by what Authority doth any one except himfelf? And what will this end in, but an univerfal Neglect of a Duty which our Maker hath required to be univerfally practifed? If it be any Scruple about the Lawfulnefs of coming to Church that keeps Perfons away, fit Opportunities fhould be fought with great Care, and ufed with great Prudence, to fet them right; and fuch Diffenters, for many there are, as do not think our Manner of Worfhip finful, but only prefer another, which perhaps they are often without the Means of attending upon, fhould be ferioufly entreated to confider, how they can juftify feparating from a lawful Communion appointed by lawful Authority, and even omitting all public Worfhip frequently, rather than worfhip with us. But then with whichfoever of thefe Perfons we difcourfe, not the least personal Anger must be shewn. Nothing but a Concern about their future Happiness. For by this Means if we make them no better, we shall at least make them no worse, and perhaps may leave in their Hearts what will some Time or other work there. Persons who profess themselves not to be of our Church, if Persuasions will not avail, must be let alone. But other Absenters, after due Patience, must be told in the last Place, that unwilling as you are, it will be your Duty to present them, unless they reform: and if, when this Warning hath been repeated, and full Time allowed for it to work, they still persist in their Obstinacy, I beg you to do it. For this will tend much to prevent the Contagion from spreading, of which there is else great Danger: and when once you have got them, though it be against their Inclinations, within Reach of your Pulpit, who knows what Good may follow? Different Cases may indeed require Difference of Treatment: and both the same Severity and the same Mildness, that will subdue one, will harden another. You will therefore act yourselves, and advise your Church-wardens to act in this Matter,

according

according to your Discretion. And after a Prosecution is begun, it shall still depend on your Opinion whether it shall be carried on with Rigour, or suspended a While in Hopes of Amendment. Only one Caution I would give you. Let not any Person's Threatenings, that, if he is prosecuted, he will go over to the Dissenters, move you in the least. Such will seldom do what they threaten: or if they do, 'tis better they should serve God in any Way than none: and much better they should be a Disgrace to them than to us. I must not conclude this Head without desiring you to remind your People, that our Liturgy consists not only of Morning but Evening Prayer also; that the latter is in Proportion equally edifying and instructive with the former; and so short, that, generally speaking, there can arise no Inconvenience from attending upon it, provided Persons are within any tolerable Distance from the Church: that few of them have Business at that Time of Day; and Amusements ought surely never to be preferred on the Lord's Day before Religion: not to say that there is Room for both.

But besides the public Service, your People

ple should be admonished to spend a due Part of their Sabbath in private Exercises of Piety. For this is almost the only Time, that the far greater Part of them have, for meditating on what they have heard at Church; for reading the Scripture and other good Books; for the serious Consideration of their Ways; for giving such Instruction to their Children and Families, as will make your Work both easier and more effectual. And therefore, though one would not by any Means make their Day of Rest wearisome, nor forbid Cheerfulness, and even innocent Festivity upon it, much less the Expressions of neighbourly Civility and Good-will, which are indeed a valuable Part of the gracious Ends of the Institution: yet employing a reasonable Share of it seriously at Home as well as at Church, and preserving an especial Reverence of God even throughout the freer Hours of it, is necessary to make it a Blessing to them in Reality, instead of a Season of Leisure to ruin themselves, as it proves too often.

But farther, besides your and their Duty on the Lord's Day, it is appointed, that all Ministers of Parishes read Prayers on Holydays,

days, on Wednesdays, and Fridays: and undoubtedly your Endeavours to procure a Congregation at such Times ought not to be wanting. Were I to repeat to you the strong Expressions which my great Predecessor Bishop *Fell* used, in requiring this Part of ecclesiastical Duty, they would surprise you. But I content myself with saying, that public Worship was from the very first Ages constantly performed on the two stationary Days of each Week; that all Holydays appointed by the Church were carefully observed by the Clergy, and the Number of them now is not burthensome: that where you can get a competent Number to attend at these Times, you will act a very pious and useful, as well as regular Part: that your own Houses will sometimes furnish a small Congregation; and what Success you may have with others, Nothing but Trials, repeated from Time to Time, can inform you. But they, whose Parishioners are the fewest and the busiest of all, I hope do not fail of bringing them to Church at the least on Good Friday, and Christmas Day, besides Sundays. For though in some of your Answers fwers to my Enquiries, thefe are not mentioned as Prayer Days, yet I prefume that this arofe from your taking it for granted I fhould underftand they were. But if in any Place they be not, I earneftly intreat they may: for at fuch Times there can be no Difficulty of getting a Congregation. I hope likewife, that you are not wanting in due Regard to thofe which are ufually called *State* Hlydays: and particularly, that if the public Faft, which hath been appointed thefe two laft Years, fhould be continued (as we have but too much Reafon to apprehend there will be Need) I beg you will endeavour, not only to bring your Parifhioners to Church on that Occafion; but move them to fuch inward Humiliation for their own Sins, and fuch Fervency of Prayer for this moft corrupt and wicked Nation, as may avert, if it be poffible, the juft Judgments of God which fo vifibly threaten us.

You muft have underftood, Brethren, in all you have heard, that I am not exhorting you to promote in your Parifhes a mere Form of Godlinefs without the Power. Outward Obfervances, by whatever Authority appointed,

pointed, are only valuable in Proportion as they proceed from a good Heart, and become Means of Edification and Grace. They are always to be reverently regarded, but never rested in: for Persons may observe, without the least Benefit, what they cannot omit without great Sin. The Business of your Parishioners therefore is, so to use the external Part of Religion, as to be inwardly improved by it in Love to God and their Fellow-creatures, and in moral Self-government: and your Business is to apply both your public and private Diligence, that this happy End be effectually attained. You have under your Care great Numbers of poor Creatures, living very laborious Lives in this World, and depending almost intirely on you for their Hopes of another. It is a noble Employment to direct their Behaviour and lighten their Toils here, by Precepts and Motives which lead them on at the same Time to Happiness hereafter. You will be sure of their Acknowledgements at least in Proportion as you succeed in this Work; but you will be rewarded by God in Proportion as you endeavour it. Think not therefore,

that

that I am laying Burthens upon you, but only *stirring up your Minds by Way of Remembrance*, and exhorting you so to watch for the Souls of Men as they *that must give Account, that you may do it with Joy and not with Grief.* It is very little in my Power either to increase or lessen your Duty. Our blessed Master hath fixed it; you have undertaken it: and were I to release you from ever so great a Part of it, I should only bring Guilt on myself without acquitting you at all. The Injunctions of the New Testament, infinitely stricter than any of Men, would continue to bind you as firmly as ever. Take *Heed therefore to the Ministry which you have received in the Lord, that you fulfil it.*

Having a Subject of such a Nature to speak to you upon, and being able to speak to you in a Body but once in three Years, you must not wonder if I go somewhat beyond the Bounds of a common Discourse. There are many other Things, and very material ones, relating to you as Parish Ministers, which I could have wished to mention now: But I was willing to treat first of such Matters as

belong-

belong more immediately to the Worship of God. If it please him that I live to another Visitation I shall in that proceed to the rest. Permit me now to add but one Word or two more upon a different Subject, and I have done.

Whilst we are serving Christianity here, with the Advantage of a legal Establishment and Maintenance, there are vast Multitudes of our Fellow-Subjects in *America*, their Negro-Slaves, and the neighbouring *Indians*, amongst whom the Knowledge of God is taught, and the Exercises of his Worship supported, if at all, very imperfectly, and with great Difficulty, by the Society for propagating the Gospel: the Income of which depends entirely on the voluntary Contributions of good Christians; and is now reduced so low, and burthened with such a Debt, that they find it necessary to propose, this next Year, according to the Powers of their Charter, and with his Majesty's recommendatory Letters, a general Collection, which they have not had for above 20 Years past, to enable them to go on. Application will

will probably not be made to every Parish separately. But I hope every Minister will give this excellent Design all the Assistance in his Power: such, as can afford it, either by becoming stated Contributors and Members of the Society; or at least by some occasional Benefaction in this Time of Need; and all, by recommending the Case to such of their People or Acquaintance as they have Reason to think will pay Regard to it. If any Person desires a more particular Acquaintance with the Nature and Usefulness and present Condition of this Undertaking, I have given some Account of these Matters in a Sermon at their anniversary Meeting lately published by me, and shall be ready to give any of you farther Information, who shall either now or hereafter apply to me for it, personally or by Letter.

But I must not yet conclude, without mentioning also the Society for promoting Christian Knowledge: who are carrying on the same good Work in the *East Indies*, which that for propagating the Gospel is in the *West*; and at the same time are promoting the Cause of Religion many Ways here at Home: particularly by selling at very low Rates, Bibles, Common-Prayers, and Numbers of other religious Books, chiefly of small Sizes, for the Use of the Poor. This they also are supported in by Voluntary Benefactions: to which whoever is able to contribute, will do a very good Work: and whoever can only purchase a few of their Books for the Use of his Parishioners, shall have both my best Assistance in it, and my hearty Thanks for it.

 I do not mean at all in speaking of these Things to prescribe to you the methods of your Charity: but only to lay before you two very deserving ones, which may possibly have escaped the Notice of some of you; and to endeavour, that the Cause of our Lord and Master may be served in as many Ways as it can: for you must be sensible how very great Need there is that none be neglected. By zealously making Use of such as are presented to us, we may possibly be of much more Service to others than we expect: but we shall be sure of doing infinite Service to ourselves.

ourselves. And *may God stir up the Wills of all his faithful People, that they plenteously bringing forth the Fruit of good Works may of him be plenteously rewarded through Jesus Christ our Lord*[a].

[a] Collect for the 25th Sunday after Trinity.

A CHARGE

DELIVERED TO THE

CLERGY of the DIOCESE

OF

OXFORD,

In the YEAR 1747.

Reverend Brethren,

I Cannot speak to you thus assembled, without congratulating you in the first Place on the happy Suppression of that unnatural Rebellion, which, since we met last, hath threatened our Religion and Liberties. Nor will either my Duty, or my Inclination, suffer me to omit returning you my heartiest Thanks, for the unanimous Zeal you expressed against it; and I doubt not were ready to express, even before the Exhortation to do so, which I was directed to send you, and which you received with so obliging a Regard. Your Behaviour, and that of the whole Clergy, on this trying Occasion, hath abounded with such Proofs of Loyalty and affection to the Government, under which God's Mercy hath placed and continued us, that his Majesty hath declared, he shall ever have the strongest Sense of what you have done for the support of his Throne, and gladly shew his Gratitude by any proper Methods of extending his royal Favour to you and to Religion. It may be hoped also, that our Fellow-Subjects will remember, what they owe to our long despised and reproached Labours: and learn, how essential a Part the Church of *England* is of our present Establishment. Indeed, not only the more candid of those, who thought amiss of us, have acknowledged our Merit now; but the *lying Lips* are *put to silence, which disdainfully and despitefully* spoke *against us* [a]. And let us go on, Brethren, to express the warmest and most prudent Zeal for what we doubly felt the Value of, when we feared to lose it: and so behave in this and all Respects, that *they who are of the contrary Part may be ashamed, having no evil Thing to say of us* [b]. For however imperfectly Men may do us Justice, our Reward from God is sure.

    I have recommended to you, in the Course of my former Visitations, various Parts of

[a] Psal. xxxi. 20. [b] Tit. ii. 8.

your

your Duty: First in general, as Ministers of the Gospel in a vicious and profane Age; then more particularly, as Incumbents of your respective Parishes. Under this latter Head, I began with what immediately relates to the Worship of God: and now proceed to another Point, of a temporal Nature indeed as it may seem, but several Ways connected with Spirituals; the Care you are bound to take of the Incomes arising from your Benefices. These Endowments are sacred to the Purposes of Piety and Charity: and it is neither lawful for us to employ them unsuitably ourselves, nor to let any Part of them become a Prey to the Avarice of others. The few that may appear to be larger than was necessary, are in Truth but needful Encouragements to the Breeding up of Youth for holy Orders. And where they lessened either an insufficient Number would be destined to that Service, or too many of them would be of the lowest Rank, unable to bear the Expence of acquiring due Knowledge, and unlikely to be treated with due Regard. Besides, the most plentiful of these Revenues may be well applied to religious Uses: and therefore, as they have been

dedicated,

dedicated, ought to continue appropriated, to them. But the Generality of them, it will surely be owned, are small enough: and a very great Part left so utterly incompetent, by the Ravages of former Times, that the little which remains, demands our strictest Care now. For, without it, poor Incumbents will not be able to maintain themselves decently, much less to exercise Hospitality and Charity towards others. Yet on these Things both their Spirit and their Success in doing their Duty greatly depend. And therefore how indifferent soever any of us may have Cause to be about our own Interests; we ought to consider ourselves as Trustees for our Successors. We all blame our Predecessors, if they have not transmitted the Patrimony of the Church undiminished into our Hands. Let us think then what others hereafter will say of us, and with what Reason, if we are guilty of the same Fault; and give away for ever, what we should count it Sacrilege in any one else to take from us.

Indeed some Persons imagine or pretend that the only Danger is of the Clergy's encroaching on the Properties of the Laity, not neglecting

lecting their own. And we acknowledge there have been Times, when that was the Danger. But they are long paſt: and God forbid we ſhould deſire to revive them. Placing exceſſive Wealth in the Hands of Eccleſiaſtics, would both endanger others and corrupt them: as the Examples of paſt Ages have too fully ſhewn. But the parochial Clergy of thoſe Times, inſtead of being the Authors of this Error, were the heavieſt Sufferers by it. And to renew the Attempt in theſe Days, would be Folly equal to its Wickedneſs: of which we ſhould ſo certainly and immediately be made ſenſible, indeed we are ſo univerſally ſenſible of it already, that there can be no Need of giving Cautions on this Head. All we wiſh for is, the unmoleſted Enjoyment of what clearly belongs to us, and a reaſonable Allowance of what is confeſſedly requiſite for us, in order to attain the only Ends of our Inſtitution, the preſent and future Happineſs of Mankind. In how many and ſad Inſtances we fail of poſſeſſing in Peace ſuch a competent Proviſion, I need not ſay. Let us all behave under whatever

Usage we receive, with the Innocence and the Prudence, which our Master enjoins. But we shall be wanting in both, if we wrong ourselves, and those that will come after us, by improper voluntary Diminutions of what is allotted for our Support: which, through Inconsiderateness and Indolence, hath been often done: designedly, I would hope, but seldom. And we may be guilty of it, either at coming into our Benefices, or during our Incumbency on them, or when we quit them: to which three Heads I shall speak in their Order.

Yet indeed, as I am now directing my Discourse to Persons, most of them already possessed of Benefices, it may seem too late to give Cautions respecting the Time of entering upon them. But all who have acted right then, will at least hear with Pleasure their Conduct approved. If any have acted wrong; which I do not know, that any of you have; on being shewn it, they may repent of it, they may consider how far they can undo what they have done, or prevent the bad Consequences that are likely to flow from it.
And

And both Sorts may be influenced more strongly, to take no improper Steps on any future Occasion, and to warn their Friends against such Errors.

I proceed therefore to say that Benefices ought neither to be given, nor accepted, with any other Condition or Promise, than that of doing our Duty in Relation to them. This Engagement is always understood, whether it be expressed or not: and no other should either be required or complied with. For when Bishops, originally the sole Patrons, to encourage the Endowment of Parishes, gave others a Right of presenting fit Persons to them; or that Right was confirmed or granted by the civil Power: they must be supposed to give it only to be exercised for the future, as it had been before: when whoever was appointed to any Station in the Church, enjoyed the Benefit of all he was appointed to, so long as he behaved well. And therefore attempting to bring the Clergy into a worse Condition, is Usurpation: and submitting to the Attempt, is encouraging Usurpation.

Yet

Yet there is a great Difference between the Things to which our Submission may be demanded. Some are grosly and obviously unlawful. If for Instance any Person, in order to obtain a Benefice, promises to give up such a Part of the Income, to connive at such a Lessening of it, to accept of such a Composition for it, to allow such a Pension or make such a Payment to any one out of it: these Things are in Effect the same with laying down beforehand such a Sum for it: which is the nearest Approach, excepting that of bribing for holy Orders, to his Sin, who thought the *Gifts of God might be purchased with Money*, and was answered, *Thy Money perish with thee*[c]. Nor can it take away, if it alleviate the Guilt, that the Payment or Pension, thus reserved, is allotted to Uses really charitable. Still it is buying, what ought to be freely bestowed: this forced Charity must disable a Man from voluntary Almsgiving, in Proportion to its Amount: and one Compliance in a seemingly favourable Instance, will only make Way for another in a more doubtful Case, and so on without End. Another Excuse I hope No-

[c] Acts viii. 20.

body

body will plead; that Obligations of this Kind may be safely entered into, since they are notoriously void. For we can never be at Liberty to make an Agreement, merely because it is so bad a one, that neither Law nor Conscience will let us keep it.

But supposing a Person binds himself to his Patron, only that he will quit his Benefice, when required: even this he ought not to do. For he hath no Right to promise it; and no Power to perform the Promise. Whoever undertakes the Care of a Living, must continue that Care till the Law deprives him of it, or his Superior releases him from it[d]. Therefore he can only subject himself to a Penalty which another may exact at Pleasure, unless he doth what of himself he is not able to do, and knows not whether he shall obtain Permission to do. Can this be prudent? Can it be fit? If he pay the Penalty, he gives Money to the Patron, though not for his first Possession of the Benefice, yet for his Continuance in it: besides that he must either distress himself, or defraud

[d] See Stillingfleet on Bonds of Resignation, in the third Volume of his Works, p. 731.

Religion

Religion and Charity of what he ought to have beſtowed on them. If then to avoid paying it, he begs Leave to reſign; he puts his Biſhop under very unreaſonable Difficulties: who by refuſing his Requeſt, may bring great Inconveniencies on the poor Man: and by granting it, may loſe a Miniſter from a Pariſh, where he was uſeful, and ought to have continued: may expoſe himſelf to the many bad Conſequences of having an improper Succeſſor preſented to him. At leaſt he will encourage a Practice undoubtedly wrong and hurtful in the Main, whatever it may be in the Inſtance before him. And why are not theſe ſufficient Grounds for a Denial; ſince whatever the Incumbent ſuffers by it, he hath brought upon himſelf?

Beſides, in Bonds to reſign, where no Condition is expreſſed, ſome unfair Intention almoſt always lies hid. For if it were an honeſt one, why ſhould it not be plainly mentioned, and both Sides cleared from Imputations? Aſſuredly unleſs Perſons are to a ſtrange Degree inconſiderate, this would be done if it could. The true Meaning therefore too commonly is, to enſlave the Incumbent

cumbent to the Will and Pleasure of his Patron, whatever it shall happen at any Time to be. So that, if he demands his legal Dues; if he is not subservient to the Schemes, political or whatever they are, which he is required to promote; if he reproves such and such Vices; if he preaches, or does not preach, such and such Doctrines; if he stands up for Charity and Justice to any one when he is forbidden: the Terror of Resignation, or the Penalty of the Bond, may immediately be shaken over his Head. How shamefully beneath the Dignity of a Clergyman is such a Situation as this! How grievously doth it tempt a Man to unbecoming, and even unlawful Compliances! What Suspicions doth it bring upon him of being unduly influenced, when he is not! Or however he may escape himself, what a Snare may his Example prove to his poor Brethren of weaker Minds, or less established Characters!

To prevent these Mischiefs, both the ancient Laws of other Churches, and those of our own* still in Force, have strictly forbidden

---

* *Stillingfleet* in his Letter about Bonds of Resignation in Miscell. Discourses, P. 42. &c. shews several Sorts of Contracts

forbidden such Contracts[f]. Particularly the Council of *Oxford*, held in 1222, prescribed an Oath against *Simony*, for so it is entitled, by which every Clerk shall swear at his Institution, that he hath entered into no Compact in order to be presented[g]. And Archbishop *Courtney*, in his Injunctions to all the Bishops of his Province in 1391, condemns those, as guilty of Simony, who, before Presentation, engage to resign when required[h]; and appoints all Persons insti-

---

tracts that are allowed; and objects not against Trusts and Confidences; [as indeed I have been assured that Dr. *Bentley* held a Living in 'Trust for the Bishop's Son] nor against what is done, in Consideration of Service, without a Compact: but only against a legal Obligation on the Party, before his Presentation, to perform such a Condition; and if he do not, to resign.

[f] The Council of *Westminster*, 1138, appoints that when any one receives Investiture from the Bishop, he shall swear that he hath neither given nor promised any Thing for his Benefice. Spelm. Vol. 2. P. 39. apud Gibson Cod. P. 845.

[g] The Words are, *quod propter præsentationem illam nec promiserit nec dederit aliquid præsentanti, nec aliquam propter hoc inierit pactionem:* where *hoc* most naturally refers to *negotium præsentationis* understood.

See *Conc. Oxon.* C. 18. in *Wilkins*, Vol. 1. P. 588. and *Lyndwood*, L. 2. *de Jurejurando*, cap. *præsenti*, in *Wake*'s Charge 1709. P. 34. and *Stillingfleet* on Bonds, &c. P. 721. and Letter about Bonds, P. 39.

[h] But it appears, by the Preamble, that it was designed only against putting it thus in the Patron's Power to dispose of the Profits, or turn the Incumbents out, and give Pluralities of Livings to such as he favoured.

tuted,

tuted, to be sworn[i], that they have not given, to obtain Presentation, either Oath or Bond to resign[k]. Again, the Constitutions of Cardinal *Pole*, when Archbishop, in 1555, censure, as being simoniacal, all Bargains or Promises for procuring of Benefices; and assert that Benefices ought to be given without any Condition, and order that the Person presented shall swear, he hath neither promised, nor given, nor exchanged, nor lent, nor deposited, nor remitted, &c. any Thing, nor confirmed any Thing given before[l]. And a Convocation held under him, two Years after, complaining that, of late Years, Persons have procured Benefices *et Prælaturas*, [Parish-Priests are *prælati*: see *Index* to *Lyndwood* in *Prælatus*:] not only vacant, but likely to become so, *non precibus & obsequiis tantum, sed & apertis muneribus*, so that *electionum saluberrimæ formæ quæ per canones liberæ esse deberent, vel fraudibus obtenebratæ*

---

[i] *Wilkins*, Vol. 3. P. 216. *Wake*, P. 35, 36.

[k] The Injunctions of *Ed.* 6. in 1547, appoint that such as buy Benefices, or come to them by Fraud or Deceit, shall be deprived, &c. And such as sell them, or by any Colour bestow them for their own Gain or Profit, shall lose their Right of presenting for that Time. *Wilkins*, Vol. 4. P. 7, 8.

[l] *Wilkins*, Vol. 4. P. 124, 125.

sunt,

sunt, vel ad compromissi necessitatem redactæ: directs, that Bishops prevent these Things, and take Care by themselves and their Officers, especially *quos in prælatorum electionibus tanquam directores & consultores interesse continget,* that *fraudes & pactiones* be excluded: and if any one have got, *per pecuniæ & munerum sordes, prælaturam vel beneficium ecclesiasticum,* he be punished [m]. It is indeed true, that the great Evil, at which these several Directions were levelled, was giving or promising *Money* for Presentation, or receiving it for Resignations [n]. And therefore it may be argued, that where no Mo-

---

[m] *Wilkins,* Vol. 4. P. 165.

[n] The Tenor of them shews this. Particularly the corrupt Resignations were to get Pensions out of Benefices, or Money for quitting them, or Exchanges gainful to the Patron or his Friends. The *Ref. Leg. Eccl. Tit. de Renunciatione,* Cap. 3. forbids only Resignations for Consideration of Gain. See *Wake,* P. 48. And Tit. *de admittendis ad Beneficia Ecclesiastica,* C. 24. only obliges a Person at Institution to swear that he neither hath given nor promised, nor will give, any Thing. And Tit. *de beneficiis conferendis* forbids only Compacts by which Benefices are lessened. See *Wake,* P. 36. who goes too far in saying the Words are general against all Manner of Contracts or Promises. The Preamble of the Oath in Can. 40. condemns only *buying and selling* of Benefices. The Latin is *Nundinatio.* But *Stillingfleet* saith, P. 719, this takes in any Benefit accruing to the Patron, because *nomine emptionis & venditionis intelligitur omnis contractus non gratuitus.*

ney is directly paid, or taken, or covenanted for, nothing illegal is done. But the Opinions delivered, and the Judgments pronounced, by the Canon Lawyers, plainly extend the Prohibition to whatever is equivalent to Money°. And it hath been urged that by how much foever a perfon leffens the Value of a Benefice to himfelf by a Bond of Refignation to the Patron in order to procure it, as unqueftionably fuch a Bond doth leffen it, fo much in Effect he pays to obtain it ᵖ. Or allowing, that in fome Cafes this doth not hold: yet Nothing will prevent unlawful Contracts in many Cafes, but prohibiting in all Cafes abfolute Contracts to refign upon Demand; which therefore the abovementioned Conftitutions have rightly done. And as the Oaths, prefcribed in them, exprefs the Denial of having made fuch a Contract; the Oath prefcribed at this Time muft naturally be underftood to imply the fame Thing. For its being lefs explicit is

---

° See *Wake*, P. 18, 24. *Stillingfleet*, P. 719, 722. and Letter about Bonds, P. 46. &c. The Injunctions of *Ed*. 6. forbid Patrons felling Livings, or by any Colour beftowing them for their own Gain and Profit. *Wilkins*, Vol. 4. P. 7, 8.

ᵖ *Stillingfleet*, P. 722.

no Proof, that, what in common Acceptation came under the Name *Simoniacal* before, doth not come under it still.

However, we must acknowledge, that Bonds of Resignation on Demand have been declared by the temporal Judges valid, and not simoniacal [q]. And they are indeed the proper Judges, whether they are such by the Common and Statute Law. But whether the Ecclesiastical Law permits them, is not so clearly within their Cognizance. Indeed all Questions about this crime seem to have been entirely out of it [r], till an Act was made,

---

[q] *Stillingfleet*, P. 735, &c. *Wake*, P. 49, &c. Indeed *Stillingfleet*, P. 735. says that the Court, having given Judgment for such a Bond in the Case of *Jones* and *Lawrence*, 8 *Jac.* 1. held, seven Years after, *viz.* 15 *Jac.* 1. in the Case of *Paschal* and *Clerk*, that it was Simony within the Statute; and he cites *Noy*, 22. for it. But *Wake* mentions not this: and *Watson*, C. 5, P. 40. says it doth not appear by the Roll that there was such a Trial; and if there was, it is of no great Authority, nor hath been regarded since.

[r] See *Wake*, P. 39, 5º. The Preamble of 5 *Eliz.* C. 23. compared with § 13. sufficiently intimates that Simony is an Offence appertaining merely to the Jurisdiction and Determination of the Ecclesiastical Courts and Judges. Yet *Stillingfleet*, P. 718 cites from *Croke, Car.* 361. the Judges as saying, in the Case of *Mackaller* and *Todderick*, that the Common Law before 31 *Eliz.* took Notice of a simoniacal Contract. But *Coke* in *Cawdrie*'s Case, 5th Rep. Fol. 8, 9. as cited by *Wake*, P. 50. puts Simony among the Crimes the Conusance whereof belongs not to the Common but Ecclesiastical

made 31 Eliz. C. 6. which *for the avoiding of Simony and Corruption in Presentations and Collations,* inflicts Penalties on those who shall either give or procure them for any Sum of Money, Profit or Benefit; or for any Promise, Bond, or Assurance of it, directly or indirectly: but at the same Time allows the ecclesiastical Laws to punish the same Offences which the Act doth, in the same Manner as they did before. Now making these Provisions is not saying, that Nothing shall be deemed simoniacal by the spiritual Judge, but what the temporal Judge shall think is forbidden by this Act[a]. And therefore, though the latter

may

Ecclesiastical Law, and repeats the same. P. 40. And *Croke,* Fol. 789. says that the Judges in the Case of *Baker,* 42 *Eliz.* held that it appertains to the Spiritual Court to determine what is Simony, and not to this Court to meddle therewith.

[a] *Stillingfleet,* P. 718. saith " the Words Simony or si- " moniacal Contract are never mentioned in this Statute." And *Wake,* P. 50. cites *Noy,* Rep. Fol. 25. as saying that " in it there is no Word of Simony; because by that Means " the Common Law would have been judge what should " have been Simony, and what not." And *Stillingfleet,* ibid. allows, that, if the Word had been there, the Judges would have had sufficient Reason to declare what was Simony and what not. Now in Truth that Part of the Act which relates to the present Affair begins thus. " And for
" the

may apprehend abſolute Bonds of Reſignation to be conſiſtent with the Statute; yet the former may juſtly apprehend them to be inconſiſtent with the Conſtitutions of the Church, which we ought to obey; and with the Oath againſt Simony, which ought to be taken in the Senſe of thoſe who originally enjoined and ſtill adminiſter it; and not to have its Meaning changed on the ſuppoſed Authority of their Opinions, who neither have undertaken to interpret it, nor, if the Judgment of their Predeceſſors be allowed, have a Right to do it.

At leaſt refuſing ſuch Bonds, on Account of the Oath, muſt be the ſafeſt Side: eſpecially, as the greateſt Divines of this Church have declared againſt them; and I think

" the avoiding of Simony and Corruption in Preſentations, Collations, and Donations of and to Benefices, &c. and in Admiſſions, Inſtitutions, and Inductions to the ſame, be it further enacted, that, if any Perſon, &c." This may ſeem to imply that no other Things but thoſe mentioned afterwards were Simony: otherwiſe the Act would provide only for avoiding ſome Sorts of Simony. Accordingly *Gibſon* Cod. P. 839. and *Stillingfl.* Pref. P. 714. and Diſ. P. 718. think it only means to puniſh ſome particular remarkable Sorts ſpecified in it: and *Wake* agrees that it abrogates no eccleſiaſtical Law. And this agrees with what is obſerved here, Note ⁿ. But ſtill the Judges: after this Act, thought that judging of Simony did not belong to them. See here, Note ʳ.

none for them. Though indeed, were the Oath out of the Question; the Bonds are apparently so mischievous, as to be for that Reason alone sufficiently unlawful. It may be said, that if the Patron attempts to make any ill Use of them, Equity will relieve the Incumbent. But I have shewn you, that their Consequences must be very bad, whatever Use the Patron makes of them. And besides, how expensive, indeed how uncertain, this pretended Relief will be; how seldom therefore it will or can be sought for; and how much better on all Accounts it is to avoid the Need of it; every one must perceive.

But let us now suppose, that a seemingly reasonable Condition were expressed in these Bonds: for Instance, to resign when such a Relation or Friend of the Patron's comes to the Age of being presented, who perhaps hath been educated with a View to the Benefice vacant[t]. Now I do not say but a

Person

---

[t] *Stillingfleet*, P. 716. supposes this to be the Intent, with which an absolute Bond is required; and saith, it is a Case, wherein a Bond may be thought far more reasonable than in others. But he expresses no positive Approbation of it; nor doth he mention there giving a Bond with this Condition

Person may very lawfully, and sometimes very charitably, from an Intention of resigning at such a Period, if Circumstances then should make it proper; and may also signify such Intention beforehand. But if he bind himself to it absolutely, besides the Distrust of him, which requiring this implies, perhaps when the Time comes, the young Person will refuse to take the Benefice, or the Patron to give it him; and yet the Incumbent must continue in perfect Dependance thenceforward: for his Case is become the same, as if his Bond had been originally without any Condition. Besides, this Contrivance for procuring an immediate Vacancy at such a particular Time, encourages Persons, even of low Rank, to purchase Patronages, separate from

---

dition expressed. But, in P. 736. he hath that Case in View where he saith, " that there may be a lawful Trust in such a " Case, I do not question:" yet adds, " but whether the " Person who takes this Trust can enter into a Bond and " take the Oath, I very much question:" And *Wake*, though in P. 22. he names this as one of the most favourable Cases that can be desired, condemns it notwithstanding; as an Obligation, which the Patron has no Right to impose, nor the Clerk any Power to enter into; as contrary to the Cannons, and the Authority of the Bishop, and the Oath of yielding him canonical Obedience, and of doing what in the Clerk lies to maintain the Rights of his See; but he doth not say it is contrary to the Oath against Simony.

the

the Manors on which they were anciently appendant, merely to serve interested Purposes. And the Generality of these, instead of considering their Right of Presentation as a spiritual Trust, to be conscientiously discharged, will of Course look on it as a temporal Inheritance, which since they have bought, they may fairly sell, at any Time, in any Manner, for what they can: or at best merely as the Means of providing a Maintenance for such Persons as they please: who therefore, unless they will be cast off intirely by their Friends, must, when they are of Age, however unfit for the Cure of Souls, however averse from it, submit to be presented, and perhaps cannot be rejected. Then further, in Proportion as this Custom prevails, Benefices, and particularly the more valuable ones, coming to be of a temporary and precarious Tenure, contrary to what they were intended; Persons of Character and Abilities, and a proper Spirit, will not so often care to take them. Or if they do, they will not usually, indeed it cannot so well be expected they should, either defend the Rights of them, or exercise Hospitality and Charity

upon

upon them, in the same Manner, as if they were to hold them for Life. Nor will the People, generally speaking, respect those who come in thus, and must behave, and go out again thus, as they ought always to respect their Ministers.

But still Persons may plead that whatever is objected against other Engagements from Incumbents to Patrons, yet if they engage only to be constantly resident, to do faithfully the whole Duty, which the Laws of the Church enjoin them, or perhaps somewhat more; this must be allowable. And doubtless it is, provided the Engagement be only a sincere Promise of acting thus, as far as they can with reasonable Convenience. Nay if they bind themselves by a legal Tie, to do any Thing, which either belongs of Course to their Benefice, or hath by ancient Custom been annexed to it, learned and judicious Authors justify them [u]. But covenanting thus to do even a laudable Action, as teaching School, or prescribing to the sick, if their Predecessors were not, without a Covenant,

[u] *Wake*'s Charge, 1709. P. 24.   *Stillingfleet*'s Letter, P. 54.

obliged to it, hath been held unlawful and fimoniacal[w]: becaufe it is promifing to fave, which upon the Matter is promifing to give, fo much Money either to the Patron, or however to thofe for whom he interefts himfelf. And indeed, though Perfons were to promife only what in Confcience they are antecedently bound to; yet if they tie themfelves either to do this, or to refign; whenever they fail in any one Part of it, as to be fure they will in fome, fooner or later, though perhaps very innocently; fuppofing the Rigour of their Bond infifted upon, (as who can fay it will not?) they are at the Mercy of the Patron ever after. He becomes their Ordinary; and is vefted, by their Imprudence, with a much greater Authority than the Bifhop hath: an Authority of reftraining their Liberty, where the Wifdom of the Church hath not reftrained it[x]: an Authority of proceeding fummarily; and depriving them, for whatever Failures he hath thought fit to infert in the Bond, without Delay and without Appeal: and this Authority he may exercife ever after, when he

[w] *Wake*, P. 18.   [x] *Wake*, P. 25.

pleafes,

pleafes, to juft the fame Purpofes, as if they had covenanted at firft to refign when requefted.

Still, without Queftion, many good Perfons have both required and given Bonds of Refignation of thefe latter Sorts: and in many Cafes, as no Harm at all hath been intended, fo no particular Harm hath been done by them. But in fo many more there hath, and it is fo neceffary to go by general Rules; and one fpecious Exception doth fo conftantly produce others that are a little lefs fo; till at laft the moft pernicious Practices creep in [y], that there is abundant Reafon to refufe making any Contracts whatfoever in order to obtain Prefentation: and more efpecially there is Reafon to refufe them, on Account of their mifchievous Influence on the Revenues of the Church: which was the immediate Occafion of my fpeaking of them now; though I thought it by no Means proper to omit the other Arguments againft them.

Perhaps it may be faid: if Patrons will have Bonds of Refignation, what can Clergy-

[y] *Wake*, P. 25.

men do? I answer, If Clergymen will not give them, how can Patrons help themselves? They must present without them, or their Right must lapse to the Bishop, who will. It may indeed be replied, that though one Person rejects the offer, another will accept it: and therefore he may as well. But this would equally be an Excuse for the worst of wrong Compliances in every Kind: and consequently it is an Excuse for none. Besides, it may happen, that by arguing with Patrons against such Contracts, they may be convinced; and learn so just an Esteem for those, who refuse them decently and respectfully, as not only to present them with double Pleasure, but do them afterwards greater Services, than they intended them before. At least whatever Clergyman behaves in so worthy and exemplary a Manner, will assuredly, if the rest of his Conduct be suitable to that Part, either by the Care of God's Providence, be raised in the World some other Way; or, by the Influence of God's Spirit, be made easy and happy in his present Situation.

But it may be objected further, that Bishops
argue

argue with an ill Grace against Bonds at Presentation, while they themselves take them at Institution. And it must be owned, that in several Dioceses, particularly that of *Lincoln*, out of which this was taken, and of *Peterborough*, which was also taken from thence [z], there is an ancient and immemorial Custom, (Customs, you are sensible, not being the same every where;) for the Clerk presented to indemnify the Bishop and his Officers from all Suits at Law for instituting him. And accordingly in this Diocese, Bonds appear to have been taken for that Purpose at all Institutions for 120 Years past: within which Time, there have been nearly, if not quite, 700 given, that are now lying in the Registry: And hence we may presume the Practice hath been the same from the Erection of the See. The Original of it probably was, that a Commission of Inquiry being formerly sent out, as old Registers prove, upon every

---

[z] In *Lincoln* Diocese they are taken only when the Bishop hath any the least Suspicion about the Patronage: in *Peterborough* and *Litchfield* always: in *Canterbury* whenever a new Patron presents: in *Gloucester* and *Exeter* they were taken till the Time of the present Bishops.

Va-

Vacancy[a] alledged, to certify the Bishop, whether the living was really vacant, who was at present the true Patron, and whatever else it was requisite he should know in order to institute: and the Expence of this Commission, and of the Proceedings upon it, being of Necessity considerable to the Clerk, who bore it[b]; the cheaper Method of a Bond from him to save the Bishop harmless, was substituted in its Room. And a further Reason might be, that, the Bishop having 28 Days allowed him, after the Presentation was tendered, to consider and inform himself, whether he should institute the Clerk presented or not; the Clerk was willing and desirous, rather to indemnify the Bishop, if he would consent to institute him sooner, than to bear the Inconvenience, and perhaps Charges, of waiting to the End of that Time.

[a] That it was on every Vacancy appears from Archbishop *Stratford's* Constitution, *Sæva*, A. D. 1342. in *Lindw.* P. 222. and from *Lindw.* P. 217. on Archbishop *Peckham's* Constitution *per nostram provinciam* verb. *Inquisitionem*, and from Bishop *Gibson's* Codex, P. 857.

[b] It appears from the above Constitution of *Stratford*, that the Clerk paid for the Commission, and therefore of Course for all that was done upon it.

At least the only Design of this Bond was and is, that if the Clerk's Title to Institution be questionable, the Bishop may not suffer by granting it. Now a Covenant for this End is surely a very lawful one, and subject to none of the Mischiefs, which, I have shewn you, attend Bonds to Patrons. Nor was any Constitution of Church or State ever pointed against it: nor I believe hath any Harm ever happened from it.

But I must own too, that there is another Condition added to these Bonds, that the Clerk shall resign his Benefice, if required by the Bishop, in Case any Controversy arise, whether his Institution be rightful. But this Provision is, in the Bond, expressed to be made only for the same Purpose with the former, the Indemnification of the Bishop: and the Penalty of the Bond is so moderated, as to serve that Purpose and no other. Accordingly I have not heard, that any one Person hath ever scrupled, in Point of Conscience, to enter into this Engagement; the Meaning of it being only, that if he prove to have no Right, he shall quit: nor indeed, that any one

one hath found Cause to scruple it in Point of Prudence. For as you may be sure the fulfilling it would never be required without Necessity; so I believe it hath never yet been required at all. That neither the Intention of this Covenant was bad, nor the Reasons for it contemptible, you will readily allow, on being told, that it began to be inserted constantly in this Diocese, at the Time when our present most Reverend Metropolitan was placed over it: which seeming Innovation was indeed only conforming more exactly to the old Example of our Mother See[c]. But still as it is a Condition, the insisting on which, in some Cases, might have bad Effects, that were not foreseen[d]; though in such Cases it probably never would be insisted on, as it never hath: I have determined, with his

---

[c] I have seen a Bond from the Bishop of *Lincoln*'s Registry with this Covenant in it, printed in the Time of *Jac.* 2 and the Bishop informs me the Covenant hath been used ever since the Restoration; how much sooner he knows not.

[d] *e.g.* A Suit may be begun which would have proved ineffectual. Yet if the Incumbent resign, the Expence of a fresh Presentation and Institution will at least be necessary for him: but indeed the Patron may present another: and in the Case of alternate Patronage, another will present.

Grace's intire Approbation, to omit it for the future.

And in every Thing, I shall not only be careful to make your Burthens no heavier, but if it can be shewn me, that I am able to do it, with Justice and Equity, I shall be glad to make them lighter. The Fees taken of the Clergy in this Diocese, whether at Institutions or Visitations, are not varied in any one Article from those, which were returned to, and not disapproved by, a Committee of Parliament in the Time of my Predecessor. They are the same, as he informs me, with those taken in the Time of his Predecessor. Nor have I hitherto found Proof, though I have inquired with some Care, that they have been increased at all materially since the Bishopric was founded [c]. Those of Visitation I am sure have not in the least. And yet the Diminution of the Value of Money in that Interval hath reduced the same Sum in Name and Quantity, to perhaps not a Fourth of what it was in Effect and Use: on which Ac-

[c] *i. e.* Allowing each of the new Instruments that are required, to cost as much as each of the old ones.

count

count proportionable Augmentations of Fees have been made, I believe, in all temporal Courts and Offices; and ancient Rules to the contrary have been justly deemed obsolete, the Reasons of them having ceased. So that where this hath not been done, or not to any considerable Degree, there is Cause to render to all their Dues with great Satisfaction.

And here I must take the Freedom of speaking to you about some Dues owing to myself, Synodals and Procurations. The former are an ancient Acknowledgment of Honour and Subjection, reserved by the Bishops of the Western Church, as long ago as when they settled their own Share of the Tithes, in each Parish, to be the future Property of the several Incumbents: And it took its Name from being usually paid at the Synodal Meetings. Now so small a Tribute, especially if considered as a Quit Rent for so great a Concession, can surely never be thought a Hardship. The other, Procurations, are also a Payment several hundred Years old, succeeding in the Place of a much more expensive Obligation, that of entertaining the Bishop and his Attendants, when he visited each

each Parish. Neither of them hath been increased since their first Beginning: the Right to both is indisputably legal: and as I am sworn to maintain all the Rights of my See, I promise myself none of you will force me to do it in a Way, that cannot be more disagreeable to you, than it will to me. If any one pleads, that complying with the Demand of so trifling a Sum will be inconvenient to him, it shall be more than returned him. If any one doubts, whether it is incumbent on him or not: his Reasons for the Doubt, whenever he lays them before me, shall be impartially considered, and allowed their full Weight. But I hope no Person will think it either decent or just, merely to refuse, without assigning a sufficient Cause: and Disuse for some Years is not sufficient, in a Matter, like this, of common Right. Most of my Clergy have very punctually shewn me this little Mark of their Regard, amongst many greater. Whether any here present have omitted it, I do not know. But I trust you with all have the Candor to think I have mentioned it, not from any wrong or mean Motive, but because I apprehend it my Duty,

and

and have not the leaft Doubt of your Willingnefs to be informed or reminded of every Part of yours.

And with this Kind of Digreffion I muft conclude for the prefent. If God prolong my Life and Health to another Opportunity, I fhall proceed to the Remainder of the Subject. In the mean Time, I heartily pray him to direct and blefs you in all Things.

A CHARGE

DELIVERED TO THE

CLERGY of the DIOCESE

OF

OXFORD,

In the YEAR 1750.

Reverend Brethren,

IN the Course of my former Visitations of this Diocese, I have recommended to you various Parts of your Duty, as Ministers of the Gospel in general, and of your respective Parishes in particular. After Things, more immediately and intirely of spiritual Concern, I proceeded, in my last Charge, to the Care, that you are bound to take of your Temporalties; with which you are intrusted, partly for the Service of Religion in your own Times, partly for your Successors, as your Predecessors were for you: a Trust, which if any of them broke, or neglected, you are too sensible they did ill, to be excusable to your own minds, if you imitate them. And dividing this Care into the Behaviour, that is requisite at your coming into Livings, during your Incumbency on them,

them, and when you are to quit them: I went through the first of these Heads; giving you proper Cautions, more especially against making any Contract or Promise inconsistent with the Oath then required of you, or prejudicial to your own Benefices, or the common Interests of the Clergy. Therefore I now go on to the second, the Vigilance, with which you ought each to superintend the Revenues and Possessions of your Church, whilst you continue Minister of it.

I have too much Cause, in every Thing, to be sensible of my own Unfitness to direct: but, in several Articles, relating to this Point, I am peculiarly unqualified: having little Experience in them, and a yet less Share of the proper Abilities and Turn of Mind for them. However, I ought not to omit being of such Use to you, as I can. There may be those amongst you, who are either still more unacquainted with these Matters, or at least have not considered them all in the same Light: as you must have observed, that very obvious Instances, both of Wisdom and Duty, escape the Attention of many, till they are pointed out to them.

And a Discourse, neither complete, nor possibly free from Mistakes, may notwithstanding do Service, by exciting Persons to think on the Subject, more than they have done hitherto.

Your Care, in Respect to this Subject, consists of two Parts: recovering what may be unduly withheld from your Church, and preserving what is left.

It is very unhappy, that so troublesome and invidious an Employment, as the former, should ever be made necessary: which yet it hath too often been. Glebe Lands have been blended with temporal Estates: and Pretences set up, that only such a yearly Rent, far inferior to the real Value, is payable from them. Tithes and other Dues have been denied; under false Colours of Exemptions in some Cases, and of Modus's in many. Every unjust Plea admitted makes Way for more. And thus what was given for the Support of the Clergy in all future Times, is decreasing continually; and becoming less sufficient, as it goes down to them. The Laity themselves, if they would reflect, must see, that they have by no Means any Cause to rejoice

in

in this. For, probably few of them in Proportion will be Gainers by what we lose: but the whole Body of them, wherever the Provision made for us becomes incompetent, must either make another at their own Expence, or be deprived in a great Measure of the good Influences of our Office, with Respect to this World and the next. But whatever they are, we ourselves cannot surely fail to be deeply concerned at the ill Aspect which these Encroachments bear towards Religion in Ages to come. Whoever is indifferent about it, shews himself very unworthy of what he enjoys from the Liberality of Ages preceding. And whoever is grieved at it, will set himself to consider, not how he can augment the Patrimony of the Church, where it is already plentiful; or any where, by dishonourable Methods: (you are very sensible, what Injustice and Folly there would be in such Attempts) but how he can retrieve any Part of it, which is illegally or unequitably seized and detained.

Now here the Foundation of all must be, a diligent and impartial Inquiry into the Right of the Case: for it would be absurd to
deceive

deceive ourselves; and unfair to demand of others what we are not well persuaded is our Due. Therefore to avoid both, we should ask the Opinion of skilful and upright Advisers. If this be in our Favour, the next proper Steps will be, laying our Claim, with the Proofs of it, so far as Prudence will permit, before the Person concerned; representing it, in a friendly and serious Manner, as an Affair, in which his Conscience is interested; procuring the Assistance of those, who have Weight with him, if we know any such; taking the Opportunity of his being, at any Time, in a more considerate Disposition than ordinary; pressing him, not to rely too much on his own Judgment, where it may so easily be biassed: yet forbidding him to rely on ours, if he would; and begging him to consult some other worthy and able Person; offering to pitch on one or more, if Circumstances persuade to it, whose Determination shall conclude us both: and entreating him to say, whether he would not think this, in any other Case, very reasonable. If still he cannot prevail on himself to comply: we may endeavour to lessen

the

the Difficulty, by propoſing to accept a ſmall Payment, where none hath been made of ſome Time; or a ſmall Variation, where a cuſtomary Payment is pleaded: in Hopes, that either the Deſire of enjoying, with ſome Degree of good Conſcience, the Main of what he withholds now with a bad one; or, at leaſt, that of avoiding the Coſt and Hazard of a Conteſt, may win him over.

If none of theſe Methods (which too commonly happens) will operate, after a due Seaſon allowed them for it; the only remaining Remedy is an Appeal to the Law. But here I would be far from exciting any of you to plainly fruitleſs or over-dangerous Attempts. I am very ſenſible, how unfavourable the Times are to eccleſiaſtical Pretenſions, how enormous the Expences of legal Proceedings, how ſmall the Incomes of moſt Benefices, how ſtrait the Circumſtances of moſt Clergymen: Conſiderations, that, one ſhould think, would reſtrain Perſons of any Generoſity, nay of any Compaſſion, from bearing hard upon them. But they ought not to be pleaded by any of us, to excuſe ourſelves from undertaking a neceſſary Burthen;

then; which perhaps we are as well able to support, as any, who will be likely to come in our Stead. I am sensible too, and would have you be so, that scarce any Thing is a more effectual Hinderance to our doing Good amongst our Parishioners, than the Character of being litigious; which many delight to give us: but with how little Justice, in general, one single Observation amongst several that might be alledged, will more than sufficiently shew; that of 700 Suits for Tithes, brought by the Clergy into the Court of Exchequer, which is only about one in 14 Parishes, during the Space of 53 Years, from the Restoration to the Year 1713, 600 were decided for them. It is true, our obtaining Justice against any Man, though in ever so clear a Cause, is very apt to be resented, by himself and his Friends at least, as grievous Injustice. But using the previous amicable Measures, which I have recommended, must in some Degree prevent, either severe Imputations upon us, or however the Belief of them: and if not intirely, yet, by Mildness, and Prudence, we may certainly regain in Time the Reputation,

putation, we never deferved to lofe. At leaft our Succeffors will enjoy, free from all Blame, what we recover to them: whereas if we acquiefce in the Detention of our Due, they will ftill be more likely to do fo, and thus the Lofs of it will be perpetuated. Therefore in Cafes both fufficiently plain, and of fufficient Importance, when all other Ways have been tried to no Purpofe, and the Right will be either extinguifhed, or much obfcured, by Delay; and perhaps the Example fpread further: I fee not, how we can excufe ourfelves from applying to a proper Court of Juftice, if we can hope to procure a Sentence from it, without abfolute Ruin or extream Diftrefs. For it is a mean and wicked Selfifhnefs, to hoard up Wealth, confult our Eafe, or court the Favour of our Superiors, by letting the Inheritance of the Church be impoverifhed, while the Guardianfhip of it is in our Hands.

But then we muft be doubly careful of what all Men fhould be abundantly more careful of, than moft are, that we never awe Perfons, efpecially poor Perfons, unjuftly, by threatening them with Law, into a Compliance

pliance with our Demands; and that no Difpute of this Kind ever entice us to do any Thing fraudulent, or provoke us to do any Thing ill-natured or vexatious. And particularly, if we have a Demand on any of the People called Quakers, we fhould, if we poffibly can, purfue it by that Method only, which the Act, for the more eafy Recovery of fmall Tithes, hath provided: and rather fit down with a moderate Lofs, than do otherwife. For they are a Generation, loud in their Complaints, unfair in their Reprefentations, and peculiarly bitter in their Reflections, where we are concerned: unwearied in labouring to render us odious, and furprifingly artful in recommending themfelves to the Great.

But I proceed to the lefs troublefome and difagreeable Duty of preferving what we ftill poffefs. Now to this End the moft obvious Way is, keeping the Glebe in our own Hands, and taking the Tithes and all other Dues, ourfelves: for which Reafon probably, amongft others, both ancient ecclefiaftical Conftitutions, and later Acts of Parliament, have reftrained and limited leafing of Benefices.

fices. But many are so little qualified for this, and would be so great Losers by it: and others would find it such a Hinderance to the Discharge of their ministerial Office, or the Pursuit of useful Studies: nay, where it hath been long disused, the People might perhaps be so much offended with the Novelty: that I would by no Means press doing it in all Cases, but only recommend it in proper ones. And where it is done, if a Clergyman were to attend to such Matters too closely; and, above all, were to be overwatchful and strict about small Demands: it would naturally raise a Contempt, if not Hatred of him. And therefore it will be much better to content ourselves with giving Parishioners, by prudent Instruction, a general Sense of their Obligation to pay their Dues; and by engaging Behaviour, a general Disposition to it; than to exact the minuter Sorts of them with an indecent Eagerness. But still, where Rights, that may seem inconsiderable in each particular Case, amount to more on the Whole, than it is convenient to lose; and yet will be withheld, if not insisted on: we must do it, with as good a Grace

Grace as we can; and remind Perfons, if there be Need, that fuch as make this neceffary, are indeed they, who act the mean Part: that it is no Fault of ours to require what the Law hath allotted us for our Maintenance; but a great Misfortune, that so much of it confifts in thefe petty Articles.

Whatever Tithes it will be incommodious to keep in our own Hands, we may compound for with thofe who fhould pay them, or leafe them to others. The former Way will ufually be kinder and more obliging, and fo far more eligible. Yet on the other Hand, if we chufe the latter, our Leffee will probably find it his Intereft to take them in Kind, which will preferve our Title to them in Kind: and therefore it may at leaft be expedient fometimes, in Relation to any queftionable Parts of them. But if a Tenant will rather give up fome of our Rights, than be at the Trouble of afferting them, we may be under a Neceffity of doing it ourfelves. And if we let any of our Tithes to the Proprietor of what they arife from, or to whomfoever we let our Glebe, it fhould never be for too long a Time at the same Rent: else we run a great Risque of being told, that we are intitled to Nothing more. The Person indeed, who makes the Agreement with us, cannot think so: and yet what even he may pretend to our Successors, we cannot foresee. But the Person, that comes after him, may insist on it even to Us: and though the Evil should be delayed longer, it will happen much too soon. Written Agreements, discreetly worded, may be an useful and effectual Preventive. Yet these, in Course of Time, may be lost by various Accidents: or Constancy of the same unvaried Payment be alledged as a stronger Argument on one Side, than they are on the other. And if either should prove our Case, contending at Law with any Parishioner will be a very undesirable Thing: and contending with a powerful one may be an impracticable Thing. Therefore we ought never to begin Customs, that may be dangerous: and if they are begun, even by our Predecessor's Fault, and yet more if by our own, we should think how to stop them without Delay. But the least we can do, is resolutely to refuse authorizing

rizing such Invasions, by giving any Thing under our Hands, which may but seem an Acknowledgment that what we receive is a prescript and unchangeable Payment, unless we are very well assured that the Law will esteem it such. We ought rather to lose it ourselves, than procure it by an Act, that will prejudice our Successors. Barely continuing to accept it unaltered, is doing more than enough to their Disadvantage: therefore we ought on no Account to go further; but on the contrary, labour to procure and perpetuate, if we can, such Evidence, as may be of service to them.

Nor should we be careful only to preserve our Benefices from any Diminution of Income, but also from any Addition of Expence, which would amount to the same Thing: for heavy Burthens, and very unfit ones, of riotous Entertainments in particular, and those sometimes at the most improper Seasons, have been introduced and established, in many Places, by the Inconsiderateness and Supineness of Incumbents. We shall do well, absolutely to break and annihilate such Customs, if it remains legally possible: and if not, to ufe our utmoft Influence towards procuring the Confent of the Perfons concerned, to change them into fomething elfe, lefs exceptionable and more ufeful, to be fecured to them as firmly, as may be; with a Covenant added, that they fhall be entitled to return to their old Ufage, if ever they are denied the Benefit of the new.

Provided the above-mentioned Precautions be obferved, we are much at Liberty to treat our Parifhioners as kindly, as we will: and very kindly we ought to treat them: never permitting them, if we know it, to go without any Thing, which is their Right; to pay any Thing, which is not due; or even to take any Thing too dear: always making them equitable Abatements, admitting every tolerable Excufe for their Delays of Payment; and rather chufing to lofe ever fo much by them, than with any Shadow of Juftice be accufed of Cruelty towards them. Yet when we fhew them any Indulgence, we fhould let them fee, we are fenfible of what we do for them; elfe they may impute it to our Ignorance, not our Goodnefs. And we ought not to be fo eafy with them, as to fet them

againft

against a Successor, who cannot afford to imitate us; or disqualify ourselves, by a promiscuous Kindness to all, from being especially kind to such as want. But whatever Improvements we make in our Benefices, by whatever just Means, it will be a prudent Guard against Envy, as well as a right Behaviour on other Accounts, to increase, at the same Time, either a sober modest Hospitality, for neither Excess nor vain Shew at all become our Function; or, which is yet better, and ought never to be excluded by the other, a judicious Charity; above all, to the industrious and virtuous Poor, extended to their Souls, as well as their Bodies.

For the Purpose of recovering or preserving the Rights of Vicarages, the original Endowments of them may be very useful. And these you are to seek for in the Register-Books of the Diocese of *Lincoln*, out of which this was taken. But I have collected Copies of some; and can direct you to Books, printed or manuscript, in which are Copies of others; or to that Part of the Register-Books, in which they may be found: and shall

shall gladly give any of you whatever Information is in my Power. But you must not always conclude your present Rights to be neither more nor less, than such an Endowment sets forth: both because there may be a subsequent one, with Variations; and because, where no subsequent one appears, long Custom, in particular Cases, may create a legal Presumption, that there was one, upon which that Custom was grounded.

For the same Use, in Rectories, as well as Vicarages, Terriers were directed: how anciently, I cannot say. But the 87th Canon of 1603 enjoins, that the Bishop of each Diocese shall procure them to be taken, by the View of honest Men in every Parish, to be appointed by him, whereof the Minister to be one: it specifies the Particulars, of which they shall consist, and orders them to be laid up in the Bishop's Registry. How often they shall be taken, it doth not mention. But plainly the Changes, which Time introduces, particularly in the Names of the Parcels and Abuttals of Glebe Lands, require a Renewal of Terriers at reasonable Distances. This Canon hath been observed so imperfectly, that of about 200 Parishes, of which this Diocese consists, there are Terriers in the Registry of no more than about 126: and of most of them only one: and of these, not 20, since the Year 1685. In the Convocation of 1704, Complaints were made of the like Omissions elsewhere: and in those of 1710, 1714, 1715, a Scheme was formed, that where no Terrier had been made for 7 Years then last past, (which looks as if a Repetition every 7 Years was intended[a]) the Minister should make one with the Church-wardens, or such Parishioners as the Bishop should appoint: that three intended Copies of it in Parchment should be signed by them; one to be exhibited at the Bishop's next Visitation, the second at the Archdeacon's, and the third put in the Parish Chest[b]. But these Proposals having never received the Sanction of due

[a] *Prideaux*, Directions to Church-wardens, § 99. saith, that the Bishop at every Visitation usually requires a new Terrier. Bishop *Gibson* proposes that there should be a new one where there had been none since the Restoration.

[b] See *Wilkins*, Vol. 4. P. 638, 656. It was also proposed that a Calendar should be made of those which were put in the Registry, and that they should not be delivered out, without Security given.

Authority,

Authority, are to be confidered as no more than prudent Directions: the Canon of 1603 ftill continues our only legal Rule. And I am very defirous to perform the Part, which it affigns to me. But then I muft beg your Affiftance in order to my nominating proper Perfons, that is, Parifhioners of the greateft Probity, Knowledge, and Subftance to be joined in the Work with you. Terriers indeed are of more Ufe in Caufes tried before ecclefiaftical Judges, than temporal: who will not allow the fpiritual Judicatures to be Courts of Record; but ftill, when regularly made, they will have fome Weight every where. At leaft they will be valuable and authentic Informations to your Succeffors: and probably the Parifhioners of future Times will be afhamed to infift on Claims, contrary to what they will fee inferted under the Hands of their Predeceffors, perhaps their Fathers or near Relations. But then, to produce thefe good Effects, indeed to prevent their producing bad ones, they muft be made with great Care. If there be a preceding Terrier, it muft be confulted; if it be defective, the Defects muft be fupplied: if it be accurate,
there

there muſt be no Variations from it in the new, but where they are neceſſary to render Deſcriptions intelligible; or where other Alterations have been made that require them. For contradictory Terriers will hurt, if not deſtroy, each other's Evidence. It will alſo be right to expreſs in them, what peculiar Burthens are incumbent on the Miniſter, or that there are none, as well as what Property belongs to him. But if his Right, or Obligation, to any Thing, be doubtful: either no Terrier muſt be made, till the Doubt is removed; or it muſt be ſet down there as a doubtful Point; but by no Means given up, to pleaſe any Perſon, or ſerve any Purpoſe whatever. For Terriers, that make againſt the Clergy, will do them abundantly more Harm, than ſuch, as make in their Favour, will do them Good. And laſtly, though it may be needleſs and inconvenient to employ many Perſons in drawing up a Terrier, yet the more ſign it, the better; eſpecially of conſiderable Perſons: for to omit any of them, and multiply the Names of others, will appear ſuſpicious. And as it may not

always

always be easy to procure such Hands, as you could wish; favourable Opportunities must be prudently sought and waited for; and the Work undertaken, when they offer, and not before.

Other very useful Precautions, of near Affinity to this of Terriers, are, that if any Augmentations have been made of your Benefices by Payments reserved in Church or College Leases, by the Queen's Bounty, or otherwise: or if any Agreements have been entered into, between you, or your Predecessors, and the Patron and Ordinary, for making any Exchange or Inclosures, or doing any other Act, which affects your Income, or any Part of it, whether it be confirmed by a legal Decree or not: proper Evidences of these Things should both be kept amongst your parochial Papers, and deposited in the public Office. Indeed the Law requires that Augmentations, made by ecclesiastical Bodies or Persons, be entered in a Parchment Book, to be kept in the Bishop's Registry for that End[c]. And though Acts of Parliament, passed for

---

[c] 29 Car. 2. c. 8. § 4, 5, 6.

any of the Purposes above-mentioned, may be considered as Things more notorious: yet without the same Sort of Care, the Memory of these also may be lost, or some of the Provisions made in them controverted.

There is still one Thing more, that, amongst several other Uses to which it extends, may be very serviceable to ascertain the Rights of Livings: I mean repeating from Time to Time, the ancient Practice of Perambulations: which hath been long freed from Superstition; and, if preserved also from intemperance and tumultuous Contests, the last of which Evils may be prevented by friendly Discourse beforehand with the chief Inhabitants of your own and the neighbouring Parishes: the Thanksgivings, Prayers, and Sentences of Scripture, with which the Injunctions of Queen *Elizabeth* direct it to be accompanied, will render it a very pious Ceremony: and the civil Benefits of it may be considerable. For though, without it, there seldom will arise any Question, to what Parish, Lands, that have been long cultivated, appertain: yet concerning others, in the

Whole

Whole or in Part, there often doth. And some, that are worth but little at present, may come hereafter to be of great Value.

But, besides preserving the Incomes of our Benefices from Encroachments, we are bound to preserve the Lands and Edifices, belonging to them, in good Condition. If therefore we commit Waste on our Glebe, or, through Covetousness or Negligence, impoverish it, or suffer our Tenant to impoverish it, we act dishonourably and unjustly: as also, if we permit our Dwelling-houses or Out-buildings to fall into Decay, for Want of early or sufficient Repair. A small Expence in Time may prevent the Necessity of a much larger afterwards, and thus, by neglecting it, we may hurt ourselves; which would doubtless be unwise; but designedly throwing the Burthen on our Successor deserves a harsher Name. And if we either squander extravagantly, or hoard avaritiously, what we save thus; it doubles the Fault. If mere Indolence be the Cause of our Omission; it is by no Means a good Principle; and produces Effects, as bad, as if it were a worse. Nay,

if

if we are influenced by the Defire of making only a reafonable Provifion for our Families: we have no right to provide for them by wronging our Succeffor: and perhaps depriving our Parifhioners of the Benefit of having a Minifter refident amongft them. Poffibly fome may fay, that their Executors muft account for whatever they leave out of Order: and therefore they do no Harm. But, it may be, they will leave them nothing to account with: efpecially as the common Law Prefers the Payment of other Debts before Dilapidations [d]. At leaft they well know, that the Law, though it will allow more, than Executors commonly pretend: and perhaps more, than would have prevented the Damage, if applied in Time; will not allow enough to repair it afterwards; or however not to compenfate moreover for the Expence and Trouble of taking that Remedy; and that therefore, in all Likelihood, a Succeffor, to avoid Law, will chufe rather to accept of lefs, than he ought to have. Now driving him to this, is doing him a grofs In-

[d] See *Gibfon*'s Codex, P. 791.

jury; and that very probably when he is juſt coming into the World in ſuch Circumſtances, that it will weigh heavy upon him, and may put him behind hand for a long Time. Some again will plead, that they really cannot afford to repair their Houſes. And doubtleſs the Condition of many is very pitiable, and deſerves the Aſſiſtance, as well as Compaſſion, of their richer Neighbours and Brethren. But ſtill what Reaſon is there to think, that they, who come after them, will be better able, when the Houſes are grown worſe? And what muſt it therefore end in, unleſs timely Prevention be applied? Others may alledge, theirs are in Repair; and no Dilapidations will be found, when they leave them. But are they in ſuch Repair, ſo ſubſtantial and ſo decent, as a Miniſter's Houſe ought, that belongs to ſuch a Benefice: or only juſt habitable, and patched up to hold out a little longer? Perhaps you keep your Houſe in as good a Condition, as you found it. But did you think your Predeceſſor acted well, when he left it you in no better? If not, that which was his Duty, is now yours. Theſe Things all Incumbents ought

to

to confider: but some more especially; as they who have large Benefices, and they who have two: which may be ordinarily supposed equivalent to a large one. Yet these latter, in how good Order soever they may, for their own Sakes, keep the House they usually reside in, have too often left the other to be treated as a Farmer or Tenant pleases: till it hath grown, if not ruinous, yet very unsuitable to its next proper Inhabitant. Again, rich Persons, that are possessed of poor Livings, ought peculiarly to reflect, how noble an Opportunity is put into their Hands of being Benefactors to them: by repairing, or if Need be, rebuilding, and fitting up, the Houses; and improving whatever little Space of Ground lies about them, in such Manner, as will make both comfortable to the succeeding Owners. And the very different Method, which they have sometimes taken, of living in better Habitations themselves, and letting these run into Decay, is extremely ungenerous and illiberal. Yet indeed, on the other Hand, making Parsonages or Vicarage Houses, or the Appurtenances of them, so large for their own Convenience, as to bring on afterwards too great an Expence in supporting them, would be a Mark, either of much Vanity, or little Consideration.

On this whole Subject I might, instead of Persuasion, use Authority alone. But as the latter would be much less pleasing to me: so I hope the former will be as effectual with you. Else, the Laws of the Church in this Nation, empower the Bishop, if Incumbents do not repair their Houses in a decent Manner[e], to take Cognizance of the Neglect either on Complaint or by voluntary Inquiry, and to proceed against them by ecclesiastical Censures; or, after admonishing them in vain, to make himself what Repair is needful out of the Profits of their Benefices: and what Proportion of them shall be applied to this Purpose, is left to his Discretion[f]: but the Injunctions of *H*. 8. *Ed*. 6. and *Q. Eliz*. directed a fifth[g]. And a further Constitution

---

[e] Semper tamen rationabilis consideratio sit habenda ad facultates ecclesiæ. Const. Edm. *Si Rector*; on which *Lyndwood*'s Note is, Quia in beneficio pinguiori requiruntur ædificia magis sumptuosa quam in beneficio minus pingui. Lib. 3, Tit. 27. de Eccl. ædificandis. Verb. *Facultates Ecclesiæ*, P. 251.

[f] See *Gibson*'s Codex. T. 32. C. 3. P. 789, &c.

[g] See *Wilkins*, Vol. 4. P. 5. The Ref. Leg. Eccl. Tit. de Dilapidationibus, C. 2. P. 77. directs only a 7th.

fourth Charge to his CLERGY.

of *Othobon*, publifhed in the Year 1268, exprefsly orders, that fuch a Sequeftration be made in the Cafe of Houfes fallen down, as well as decayed[h]. And the *Ref. Leg. Eccl.* had provided in the fame Manner for the fame Thing[i], in Conformity with evident Reafon. Indeed, where no Houfe hath been for a long Time, compelling the Incumbent to rebuild one may feem hard. But is it not harder ftill, that his Parifhioners and Succeffors fhould never more enjoy an Advantage, intended to be a perpetual one? At leaft, whatever he may think of his legal Obligation, he fhould confider, whether he is not in Confcience obliged to devote fome fitting Share of his Income to this Ufe. Surely, if he doth not think it a ftrict Duty, he muft think it, unlefs there be fome peculiar Reafon to the contrary, an excellently good Action. And fuppofing that what he can lay by, will amount only to a tolerable Beginning: yet others may, and probably will, fooner or later, add to it, and complete the Work,

[h] *Gibfon*'s Codex, Tit. 32. C. 3. P. 789.
[i] Tit. de Dilap. C. 2. P. 77.

But

But whatever Care you ought to take, and I ought to see that you take, in Relation to your Houses: there is still a much greater, for the same Reasons and more, due from you, who are Rectors, in Relation to your Chancels: and I am yet more expressly authorized, by Statute-Law as well as Canon, to superintend this Matter. Chancels are the most sacred Part of the Church: and the whole Church ought to be preserved in a Condition, worthy of that Being, whose it is; and fit to inspire his Worshippers with Reverence. The Light of Nature taught the Heathens to adorn their Temples [k]. God himself provided, by express and minute Directions, for the Beauty of his Sanctuary amongst the Jews: the ancient Christians imitated these Precedents, as soon as ever the Danger of Persecution ceased [l]: and if the following Ages carried their Notions of Magnificence and Ornament in religious Edifices too far, as undoubtedly they did, in heaping up Treasures there, which had much

---

[k] *Hor.* Od. 15. Lib. 2. and Sat. 2. Lib. 2. v. 103, 104, 105.   [l] See *Bingham*.

better

better have been diftributed to the Poor, than kept to provoke the Envy and Avarice of the Great: yet in this Country, for feveral Generations paft, the contrary Extreme hath prevailed to fo fhameful a Degree, as muft needs give Papifts an exceeding great Difguft to Proteftantifm; and Infidels no fmall Contempt of Chriftians, as either defpifing inwardly the Religion they profefs, or being too fordid to pay it the common outward Marks of Refpect.

Now what Hope can we have of bringing our People back, unlefs we fet them the Example? What can we fay to our Parifhioners about their Churches, or to Lay-Impropriators about their Chancels; or, fay what we will, how can it be expected they fhould mind us, if we are blameable ourfelves on the fame Head? In refpect of their Duty in this Point, and fome Concern, (indeed not a little) which you have with it, I intend to fpeak at large, if God fpare my Life and Health to another Vifitation. But at prefent I confine myfelf to what is more immediately and intirely the Province of the Clergy. Anciently the Repair of the whole Church was incumbent

cumbent on the Rector, as of common right [m]. I believe it continues to be so still in other nations: but the Custom of ours hath released us from the largest Part of the Burthen: for which Reason we ought to bear the Remainder very chearfully; and exceed what in Strictness might be demanded of us. Plainness of Appearance, though carried almost to the Borders of Neglect, in Relation to our own Persons and Abodes, may be a judicious and instructive Mark of Simplicity and Humility. But it will be much more so, if, at the same Time, we are liberal in providing for the Honour of sacred Things. And if, instead of that, we take just the contrary Part; dwell, as the Prophet expresses himself, *in ceiling Houses, and let the House of God lie waste* [n]; suffer the principal Part of it, and that with which we are intrusted, to be in a worse Condition, than any common Room we live in; think Nothing too good for ourselves, and every thing good enough for him and his Service; it is an exceeding bad Sign; and must have a most undesirable Effect on all who observe it. I believe indeed

[m] See *Const. Othob.* Tit. 17. and *John de Athon,* Verb. *Cancellis.* [n] *Hag.* i. 4.

that

that the Chancels, which belong to Incumbents, will be generally found in the best Condition of any. Yet some even of these, I fear, have scarce been kept in necessary present Repair, and others by no Means duly cleared from Annoyances, which must gradually bring them to Decay: Water undermining and rotting the Foundations, Earth heaped up against the Outside, Weeds and Shrubs growing upon them, or Trees too near them. Where sufficient Attention is paid to these Things: too frequently the Floors are meanly paved, or the Walls dirty or patched, or the Windows ill glazed, and it may be in Part stopt up, or the Roof not ceiled: or they are damp, offensive and unwholesome, for Want of a due Circulation of Air. Now it is indispensibly requisite to preserve them not only standing and safe, but clean, neat, decent, agreeable: and it is highly fit to go further, and superadd, not a light and trivial Finery, but such Degrees of proper Dignity and Grandeur, as we are able, consistently with other real Obligations. Perhaps they may have been long, or perhaps always, as mean as they are at present. But the

the Meanness which in Ages of less Elegance might give no Offence, may justly give more than a little now. And why should not the Church of God, as well as every Thing else about us, partake of the Improvements of later Times? In several of your Chancels, I doubt not, every Thing which I have been recommending is done. In others you have resolved to do it: and if any have not rightly considered the Matter before, they must be sensible that it was my Duty to admonish them, and is theirs to regard the Admonition. For, as to the Excuses, which may be pleaded under this Head of Chancels, they have been obviated, under the former of Parsonage-Houses.

It only remains now, that I speak briefly to the third Point, our Obligations in regard to the Temporalities of our Benefices, when we have a near View of quitting them: whether by Death, which may be near us at any Time, and must be so in old Age; or any other Way. Some, because they were not to continue Incumbents long, have set themselves to consult their own Interests, by Neglect of all expensive Duties, by committing

ting Waste, by allowing others to commit it. A Manner of proceeding, in all Cases unjust: when they are removing to a better Income, peculiarly dishonourable: when they see their latter End approach, shockingly wicked; unless the Decay of their Faculties furnish some Excuse for them. Rejecting therefore all such Practices with just Abomination, we are bound, in these Circumstances, to consider seriously, what our past Faults and Omissions, relating to this Article, have been: to undo, as far as we can, what we have done amiss: to do immediately what we ought to have done sooner: to make the Amends we are able, if any Harm hath happened by the Delay; and indeed, some Amends for the Chance there was, that Harm might have happened. But how rightly soever we may have acted hitherto, there will still be Duties, peculiar to the Time, which I am now supposing; that we secure to our Successors, whatever Books, Deeds, and Papers, relating to our Benefices, came down to us from our Predecessors; whatever Evidences our own Incumbency hath furnished; in a Word, whatever Notices may be of Importance, concerning

cerning the Rights, or the Value, of the Living we enjoy. But particularly, if we have been so inconsiderate, as to make any long Agreement, which a succeeding Minister may be in Danger of mistaking, or others may be tempted to set up, for an established Prescription; as may easily happen if it was done many Years ago: we ought to leave them the most authentic Proofs of the real State and Truth of the Case. Some have through Indolence omitted these Things. Others have designedly kept in their own Power, or left in that of their Executors, all such Means of Information; that their Successors, in order to receive them, may be bound to behave reasonably and kindly, as they are pleased to term it; that is, may be under a Necessity of submitting to whatever unreasonable Things shall be demanded of them; in respect of Dilapidations, or any other Point. This, you cannot but see, would be making an unfaithful Use of those Lights, which have been intrusted with you by others, and an oppressive one of those which you have added yourselves. Or supposing that only equitable Requests are made

to

to a Succeffor, and that he refufes them; ftill it is not a Chriftian Part, to prevent this Injury by threatning, and much lefs to revenge it by doing, what in all Likelihood would be a far greater Injury; and may extend its bad Effects beyond the Perfon who hath given the Provocation, to all that fhall fill his Place hereafter, though perfectly innocent; and to every one that might have fhared in the Advantage of their enjoying a more plentiful Income. Nor is it fufficient, that you difapprove fuch Conduct, unlefs you make a due Provifion, that your Reprefentatives when you are gone fhall not be guilty of it. You may have a better Opinion of them, in this Refpect, than they deferve: at leaft, there can be no Harm in taking a little more Care of fuch a Matter, than might be abfolutely neceffary.

One powerful Motive, to be careful in all the Points which I have been mentioning, is, that few Things will contribute more to your maintaining while you live, and leaving when you die, the Character of Men of Probity and Honour, amongft your Neighbours

in

in general, and your Brethren of the Clergy in particular, than your diligent and difinterefted Attention to act worthily and kindly in Relation to your Succeffors, though probably you know them not, or however have no perfonal Connection with them. Nor will many Things throw a blacker or more lafting Stain upon Perfons, than a low Cunning, or a felfifh indifference, in thefe Affairs. But indeed Confcience, as well as Reputation, is deeply concerned in the Matter, as I doubt not, but you are all fenfible. Nor furely will any one elfe imagine, either that my Exhortations to you, any more than yours to your Hearers, imply you to be guilty of, or efpecially inclined to any of the Faults, againft which they are levelled: or that, by fpeaking thus long of your worldly Affairs, I feem to think them of Weight equal, or comparable, to your fpiritual Functions. But the beft of us have Need to be admonifhed of all our Duties, be they Duties of higher Rank or lower, each in their Turns. Temporal Things are not to be neglected: and thofe leaft of all, which

are

are set apart for the Service of Things eternal. But then we must be watchful over them, in order to employ them, as they were meant to be employed: and if we preserve and transmit them ever so faithfully, but use them unfaithfully; studying only or chiefly to enrich or advance ourselves, or gratify our sensual Appetites, or Love of Diversions, or of elegant Appearance, by Means of those Revenues, which were given us for Ends widely different: (partly to make a comfortable and moderate, not a superfluous and invidious Provision for ourselves and ours, and partly to serve the Purposes of Religion and Charity) we offend God, sin against our Brethren, and provoke Men to take from us what they are too ready to say we do no Good with: as indeed little would be done, were such a Conduct general. It is true, and the Laity ought to consider it a great deal more than they do, that we have very few of us much, if any Thing, to spare. But they who have, should *let their Light shine before Men*, and be seen to lay it out in pious Uses prudently chosen:

and

and the poorest should occasionally give what Alms they can; and make Amends for their Inability on this Head, by a double Diligence in useful Instruction, pious Example, and obliging Behaviour, to the meanest of their People. Without a remarkable Degree of such Care, we shall have few or no Friends: and notwithstanding it, we shall have many Enemies. This is hard Treatment: but angry Complaints will only make it worse; and the most reasonable Expostulations not much better, unless we first consider, wherein we are faulty or defective, and amend it; wherein we are unjustly blamed or suspected, and clear ourselves; then patiently persevere in well-doing, *in all Things approving ourselves as the Ministers of God, by Pureness, by Knowledge, by Longsuffering, by Kindness, by Love unfeigned, by the Word of Truth, by the Armour of Righteousness on the right Hand and on the left, through Honour and Dishonour, through evil Report and good Report* [e]. Other Means, if they could support us, cannot enable us to answer the End of our Institution. But by

[e] 2 Cor. vi. 4, 6, 7, 8.

these we may still hope not only to confute, but which must ever be our chief Aim, if possible to convert, at least to mollify our Adversaries; and so recommend ourselves to more impartial Persons, that they may *receive with Meekness the engrafted Word, which is able to save their Souls*[p]. Or should we, after all, in Respect of ever so many, *labour in vain, and spend our Strength for Nought, yet our Judgment is with the Lord, and our Work with our God*[q].

[p] James i. 21.   [q] Isa. xlix. 4.

A

CHARGE

DELIVERED TO THE

CLERGY of the DIOCESE

OF

OXFORD,

In the YEAR 1753.

Reverend Brethren,

I Have never attempted in my former Visitations, nor shall I in this, to entertain you with any Thing new and curious: thinking it much fitter for me, and better for you, to speak to you of such Points, immediately relating to common Practice, as, though easily understood, are too frequently disregarded. With this View I have gone through the principal Parts of your Duty, as parochial Ministers, in Respect both of Spirituals and Temporals. But besides what is wholly incumbent on yourselves, in some things you are jointly concerned with your Church-wardens: and in others, though not expresly commissioned by Law to enterpose, you may do it nevertheless, with peculiar Propriety, Weight, and Influence.

Of the former Sort are thofe Offences againſt Religion and Morals, which the Church-wardens are bound by Oath to preſent; and the Incumbent, or his Curate, impowered and charged by the 113th and following Canons to join with them in preſenting, if need be; or to preſent alone, if they refuſe. This naturally implies, what the 26th Canon expreſſes, that the Miniſter is to urge the Church-wardens to perform that Part of their Office. Indeed your firſt Endeavour ſhould be, by due Inſtructions and Exhortations, to hinder ſuch Offences: your next, by due Reproofs, public or private, to amend them. But if both prove ineffectual, what remains is, to get them corrected by Authority. I am perfectly ſenſible, that both Immorality and Irreligion are grown almoſt beyond the Reach of eccleſiaſtical Power: which having in former Times been very unwarrantably extended, hath ſince been very unjuſtly and imprudently cramped and weakened many Ways. I am ſenſible alſo, that ſometimes Church-wardens, nay even Miniſters, are ſo dependent on Perſons, who deſerve to be preſented,

that

that they cannot prefent them without imminent Hazard of ruining themfelves: and farther ftill, that fome Offenders, if they were thus expofed, would only become worfe, and fet themfelves to make others worfe; while fome again, as the Apoftle expreffes it in this very Cafe, would be *fwallowed up with overmuch Sorrow*[a]. Now furely it cannot have been defigned by our gracious Redeemer, or the Rulers of his Church, that the Power of fpiritual Cenfures, which the fame Apoftle hath twice declared the Lord to *have given for Edification, not for Deftruction*[b], fhould be exercifed in Circumftances like thefe. Therefore when Circumftances are evidently and undeniably of this Kind, I think you fhould not infift on your Church-wardens prefenting. But there is much more Danger of their being guilty of too great Remiffnefs, than running into over much Rigour. And therefore you muft advife and intreat them to make Prefentments of Sinners, where probable it will be ufeful; and to contemn the Difpleafure of bad People, when it can have no extremely ill Confequences, (of which there is commonly

[a] 2 Cor. ii. 7.   [b] 2 Cor. x. 8. and xiii. 1.

much more Fear than is neceſſary; for the Hope of their Amendment and the Good of others round them. The very Office of Church-wardens obliges them to this: their Oath yet more firmly. And if they are backward ſtill, after being told it doth; you muſt acquaint them, that you are directed by the 26th Canon, (in the Execution of which however, as in all Points of Diſcipline, Diſcretion ſhould be uſed,) to refuſe them the holy Communion; not indeed for every Neglect of preſenting Offences, but if they wilfully neglect it in deſperate Defiance of their Oath, when they are urged to it by their Neighbours, their Miniſter, or Ordinary: for ſo the ſame Canon deſcribes the Caſe: in which Caſe likewiſe you will inform them, the Court is authorized, by Canon 117, to proceed againſt them for Perjury. But, along with theſe Terrors, you will be ſure to join fitting Encouragements. You will promiſe to defend them to the Pariſhioners, and even to the Perſon preſented, as doing only their duty. You will aſſure them, as you may, firſt, that the Court will take Notice of their Preſentments, no farther, than is proper; ſo that they ſhall not incur

incur the Displeasure of the Offenders and their Friends for Nothing; than, that it will proceed, not with a View to Gain, but to Reformation and Example; not with excessive, nor, if it can be avoided, with the utmost Rigour, but with Equity and Moderation.

If all this be unsuccessful, you must, in Cases that require it, offer to join with them, or even resolve to present without them. But you must never take any Step in these Matters, much less the more extraordinary Steps, from Motives of Resentment, Interest, or Party. If such Inducements can be with any Colour of Reason imputed to you, they will so grievously discredit what you do, that probably you had better do Nothing. But only take Care to shew, that you act merely from good Intention, accompanied with Temper and Prudence, after trying gentler Methods in vain: and some will vindicate, and even applaud you: more will inwardly and silently respect you: and the Number of the rest will not be formidable.

But then whoever brings a Complaint, must enable the Court to take due Cognizance

zance of it: else Presentments will be despised; and the Consequences be worse, than if they had not been made. Evidence must of Necessity be furnished: otherwise there can be no Proceeding. Expences, I hope I may promise, will be as low as possible; and they should be cheerfully born for the Good of the Parish and the Public. It is not reasonable that the Court should bear them. Temporal Courts never do. And besides, there is Room for plausible, though unjust, Suspicions of Partiality, where the Judge appears to be in Effect Prosecutor too, and is interested in condemning the Party accused.

When Persons are presented, you must use your best Endeavours to make them sorry, not merely that they are in Danger of being punished, but principally that they have sinned: and in Proportion as you succeed in that, recommend them to such Favour, as can be shewn them. When Persons are excommunicated, (which I heartily wish no one ever was but for Crimes, though indeed a wilful Contempt of Authority is a great Crime) you must press them to consider seriously, how they would be affected, if a Physician or a

Lawyer

Lawyer of Eminence pronounced their Case desperate; and of how much greater Importance the Concerns of Eternity are, than those of Time. You must also admonish them, that slighting a Censure, passed on them for their Amendment, will make their Condition still more deplorable. And when they have been denounced excommunicate, by the 85th Canon, the Church-wardens are to see, that in every Meeting of the Congregation they be kept out of the Church. Nor must you suffer them to be Sureties for Children in Baptism, to receive the holy Eucharist or to have Christian Burial. Farther, if they continue without Absolution for three Months, the 65th Canon directs you to declare them excommunicate in the Parish Church every half Year; that others, meaning such as have no necessary Connections with them, may thereby be admonished to refrain their Company, and excited the rather to procure out a Writ *de Excommunicato capiendo*: that is, if the Circumstances of the Case make it requisite. Again, when Persons do Penance, you must be diligent to make them seriously sensible
of

of the Usefulness of such Discipline; and the unspeakable Obligations they have to the Gospel of Christ, which alone assures Men of Forgiveness on any Terms. And lastly, both on all such, and all other fit Occasions, you must remind your People, that however the Censures of the Church may be relaxed or evaded, the final Judgment of God on obstinate Sinners is both unavoidable and insupportable.

Besides the Presentment of Persons who give Offence, you are concerned likewise in that of Things belonging to the Church, which are not kept in good Repair and Order.

I have already spoken to you concerning the Repair of your Houses and Chancels: and enlarged on the Reasons, why both, but especially the latter, should be always preserved not only in a firm and safe, but decent and respectable State. Now the same Reasons hold in regard to the rest of the Church: and after you have set the Example in your own Part, you may with Reputation and Weight call on your Parishioners to do what is proper in theirs. And indeed you are

bound

bound to it. For, as *John* of *Athon* hath juftly obferved [e], *Licet per confuetudinem exoneretur Rector a fumptibus præftandis, non tamen eximitur a cura & folicitudine impendendâ.* Thus far even the Body of the Church is ftill under your Infpection; and if any Thing be remarkably amifs there, and you take no Notice; good and confiderate Perfons will lament it, as a bad Sign and of bad Confequence: others will make your Indifference a Plea to excufe their own; and yet while they are glad of it, will be likely enough to condemn you for it: and perhaps be led by it to think meanly of Religion, as well as of you. Befides, Church-wardens have often but little Senfe of Propriety in thefe Matters: therefore you fhould labour to give them a Senfe of it: convince them, by Reafon and Scripture, of the Honour due to the Houfe of God: fhew them, that their own Honour too is interefted; that a Church in a handfome Condition is a Credit to the whole Parifh; and in particular to the Officers, who have put it in that Condition, and whofe Names will be long remembered on that Account. They are often afraid of the Expence. Argue

[e] *Conft. Othob.* 17. verb. *ad hoc tenentur.* P. 113.

with

with them, that Things may be done gradually, and so the Expence be rendered almost imperceptible: persuade them to lessen their Expences in needless Matters; in eating and drinking at Visitations, and on other Occasions, sometimes to Excess, never to any good Purpose; and observe to them, how much righter and more commendable it would be, to lay out or lay up that Money for proper Uses: how shameful indeed, to squander it in Riot and Folly, and be never the better, but the worse the next Day; when they might dispose of it so, as to see the good Effects for Years, and have them seen for Ages. If still you cannot influence the present Church-wardens, try their Successors. You have a concurrent Right with the Parishioners in chusing them; and if your Opinions differ, you are to chuse one, they another: unless there be a Custom to the contrary. Surely then, within some reasonable Time, you may get such as will hearken to you. If you fail of Success that Way, desire your People to reflect how their Money goes: not in Fees of Visitations, which are no higher now, than when the Value of Money

Money was thrice, perhaps five Times, higher, but in Extravagance and Intemperance: that therefore they ought not to complain of the Court, but of their own Officers; indeed ought to disallow the wrong and idle Articles of their Accounts; and may be assured, the Court will support them in doing so.

Sometimes the Church-wardens are willing to lay out the Money as they ought, but the Parishioners unwilling. In that Case you must acquaint the former, that no Man's Consent is wanted for their repairing and keeping in good Order, both the Church, and every Thing belonging to it, which is either necessary, or which they found there: nor is the Consent of every Man requisite, but of the Majority only of a Parish-Meeting duly called, for adding any Thing new, provided the Ordinary approve it. However, they should do their utmost, and you should assist them, to procure the Concurrence of all the Parishioners; or at least, of as many as possible: to whom you will represent for this End, that a moderate Expence now will prevent a much greater hereafter: that almost all the Churches in the Nation were built many Ages ago, and a very great Part of them about the fame Time: that without conſtant and ſubſtantial Repairs, in another Generation or another Century, they will be falling at the ſame Time; and how will they be rebuilt? The Inhabitants, if we may gueſs from what we ſee at preſent, will be both leſs able and leſs inclined. As for Help from Briefs: thoſe for other Things produce but little; but thoſe for Churches extremely little; to the great Shame indeed of Perſons, who call themſelves Chriſtians: and you ſhould labour to rectify their Prejudices on this Head, and excite them to be more charitable. But God knows whether they will; and if hereafter they ſhould, what can be hoped from it, when almoſt every Pariſh in the Land will want a Brief? In many, it is to be feared there will be no Churches; in others, wretchedly mean ones; to the Contempt of all Religion amongſt Infidels, and of the Proteſtant Religion amongſt Papiſts. Repeat and inculcate it therefore on your People, that they muſt take Care of the Churches they have: if not, their Poſterity

will

will run the Rifque of having none. Too many will fcarcely be moved even by that Confideration: but there is the more Need of moving fuch as you can; and, getting into a Condition of moving more, by all proper Methods of recommending the Gofpel and yourfelves.

But to Perfons of Rank and Figure in your Parifhes, one fhould hope you might apply with very fair Profpect of Succefs. To thefe you may furely reprefent at favourable Seafons, that labouring People part very hardly with the Money, which they get very hardly: that therefore their Superiors fhould not only ufe their Influence and Example to make them willing, but indeed fhould do for them what perhaps they are almoft as unable to do, as they are unwilling; efpecially what goes any Length beyond Repairs abfolutely neceffary: for that People of low Degree, though they may have fome Notion of Neatnefs and elegance, yet will murmur grievoufly to pay much for it in their Churches, and Part of their ill Humour will fall on the Doctrine taught there: that efpecially if they are Tenants, their Concern in the Place being temporary, and possibly also short or uncertain, they will of Course endeavour to shift off the Burthen from themselves: but that Landlords have a more lasting Interest, and will find their Account better in doing Things early at their own Cost, than in letting them run on, till the Cost is much greater: for then, in some Shape or other, it must come out of their Pockets. With these Considerations you will not fail to join others of a higher Nature: that sacred Fabrics are appropriated to the noblest of Uses, the Worship of the great God; and to preserve or put them in a Condition suitable to it is one very proper Method of expressing and cherishing a Sense of Piety in their own Minds, and spreading it through their Families, Neighbours and Dependants; whereas, by suffering his House to be an Object of Contempt and Scorn, while perhaps they spare Nothing to beautify their own, they will be understood, and will tempt all around them, to despise the Service performed there, and him to whom it is paid: that repairing and embellishing their Churches will employ the Poor full as beneficially, as

adorning

adorning their Seats and Gardens, and procure them a much better grounded, and more general, Esteem. Indeed it is surprising, that Noblemen and Gentlemen will squander vast Sums in the Gratification of private Luxury and Vanity, for which more condemn than applaud them; and not consider, that much smaller Sums bestowed on public Works, especially in Honour of Religion, would gain them the Admiration of a whole Country; and the peculiar Blessing of many, whom they would thus ease from Burthens: besides that they might shew their good Taste, if that be the favourite Point with them, no less in one Way than the other. But even Heathen Writers have observed long ago, that expensive personal Indulgence, and mean-spirited Parsimony in what regards the Community, are often Companions, and always ill Symptoms[d].

But you may press the Obligation of repairing and ornamenting yet more strongly, both on such of the Nobility and Gentry, and on such Colleges and ecclesiastical Persons

[d] *Cic. pro Flacco. Hor. Od. L. 2. 15. Sat. L. 2. 2. 103, 104, 105.*

or Bodies, as are Impropriators: and likewise on the Lessees of these latter; because they have a more beneficial Interest in the Estate, than the Lessors. Being possessed of the greater Share of what was originally given for the Support of the Service and the Fabric, they are bound, at least in Conscience, to take Care of both, if it be needful: but of one Part of the Fabric, the Chancel, they are indisputably bound by Law to take Care. And yet too commonly even those amongst them, who should be the most attentive to this Point, strangely neglect it; or throw it on their Tenants, who they know will of Course neglect it; and concern themselves no farther. So their Chancels are only in such Sort of Repair, as their Barns and Outhouses. Now handsome Benefactions to put them in a better Condition, given from Time to Time, and especially when good Fines are received, would shew Piety and Generosity at once; would abate the unjust Envy and Hatred, to which academical and ecclesiastical Owners of Estates are liable; and set an Example, which others might probably imitate.

I have

I have already said, in speaking of Chancels, that the Ornaments of sacred Places ought not to be light and gaudy, but modest and grave. Amongst these a very proper one, of the cheaper Kind, is, writing on the Walls chosen Sentences of Scripture. This was done as early as the 4th Century[e]: but in Process of Time ceased to be done, at least in the vulgar Tongue: and being restored at the Reformation, was forbidden, as promoting that Cause, by Bishop *Bonner* in Queen *Mary*'s Reign[f]. It not only diversifies the Walls very agreeably and decently, but affords useful Matter for Meditation to the People, before the Service begins; and may afford them useful admonition, when their Eyes and Thoughts are wandering in the Course of it. For these Reasons, I presume, the 82d Canon directs, that such Sentences be written in convenient Places; and likewise, that the ten Commandments be set upon the East End of every Church and Chapel: to which undoubtedly the Creed and Lord's Prayer, though not mentioned in the Canon, are very fit Companions.

[e] *Bing.* viii. 8, 3.   [f] *Wilkins*, Vol. iv. p. 108.

You must also endeavour, that such Care may be taken of the Furniture of the Church, and whatever is used in it, as the Canons and Rubricks, and the Nature of the Thing require: that the Surplice be originally of proper Linen, and kept clean, and renewed before it becomes contemptible by Age: that the Bible and Prayer Books be whole and unsullied, and well bound: that the Vessels for the Celebration of both the Sacraments, and the Cover of the Holy Table, but more especially the Bread and Wine placed upon it, be suitable in all Respects to the Solemnity: not such as may give Disgust to the more delicate, and tempt them to abhor, as the Scripture Expression is, *the Offering of the Lord*[z]. These are in their Kind, Points of Importance: and such as you may for the most Part easily carry. Another Thing, worthy of Notice, is the Condition of your Church-yards. I take it for granted, though I am afraid I forgot to name it, that you keep those, which belong to yourselves, neat and decent: not turning in Cattle to defile them, and trample down

---

[z] 1 Sam. ii. 17.

the Grave-stones; and make confecrated Ground such, as you would not suffer Courts before your own Doors to be; but taking the Profits of the Herbage in such Manner, as may rather add Beauty to the Place. And I hope where a Church-yard belongs to an Impropriator, you will do your best to get the same Respect paid it; and to whomsoever it belongs, the Fences well kept up.

If, in any or all of the Particulars, which I have specified, your Representations will be less offensively introduced, or your Attempts be of more Weight, for your being able to say, that I directed you to make them, I do hereby direct you accordingly; and desire you to say, that I did. Nor should you be contented with a transient Mention of the Subject once or twice; but where there is any Hope, return to it on proper Occasions, and try the Force of modest Importunity. If, after competent Trial, you find no Effect, you must urge the Churchwardens to present what is amiss, if they will do no more. Indeed such Things as belong to their own Care, they should not present,

present, but amend: and the Canons require not the former, but the latter. Only when they have not Time for the latter, the former is all they can do: and when they have, it is better than doing Nothing. For it gives Notice, and furnishes Room for Admonitions and Injunctions. If there be Need, here again you must encourage them to present, by engaging to plead their Cause with the Parishioners. You may also safely promise them, that they shall suffer no oppressive or hard Treatment, shall not be required to lay out upon any Thing more than is fitting, and shall have reasonable Time allowed, even for that. I need not say, that both to qualify yourselves for pressing them to present, and on many other Accounts, you must take effectual Care, that Nothing belonging to you be presentable. Else they will have a ready Answer for you: and it will be a sad Thing to stand in Awe and be at the Mercy of those, who ought to reverence you. If you cannot prevail on them otherwise, I apprehend you may join with them; and if you cannot prevail on them at all, I apprehend you may present
without

without them, in the Case of Repairs, as well as Offences, by Virtue of the Interpretation, which Practice hath put on the abovementioned Canon: though it speaks, I own, expresly of Nothing besides Offences. But in doing either of these Things, you must be sure to observe the Cautions given under the former Head.

Yet after all, I am well aware, that you may often have great Difficulties to encounter, possibly sometimes too great to surmount, and to diminish them for you, I have endeavoured to procure a parochial Visitation from the Archdeacon, which he hath promised. But then, for the Credit of your Parishioners and your own, let this be an Inducement to put Things in good Order, that he may find them so: not to leave them in bad Order, that he may rectify them.

Another very useful Institution, for these and many valuable Purposes, was that of Rural Deans: which took Place here before the Conquest, was kept up till the great Rebellion, was restored afterwards in several Dioceses, and particularly in this by the
admirable

admirable Bishop *Fell* [h], was found not quite extinct, and was completely revived by the late excellent Bishop of *Glocester* [i], in that County, and is preserved to this Day in some Parts of the Nation besides. These Deans, being chosen out of the resident parochial Clergy, could inspect, with small Trouble, the Churches and Parishes within their several narrow Districts; and being bound to report what they found amiss, could do it with little or no Offence. In the latter End of Queen *Anne*'s, and the Beginning of the late King's Reign, the Convocation made some Progress towards the Re-establishment and better Regulation of this Office. When that, or any other Branch of Discipline, may be the Subject of public Consideration again, is very uncertain. I should be very glad, with your Approbation, to set it up once more amongst us, in such Form as might be most beneficial and satisfactory: but contented at present with hinting the Matter, I leave and recommend it to your serious Thoughts.

---

[h] *Kennet.* Paroch. Ant. P. 653.   [i] Bishop *Benson.*

A third Particular, of confiderable Importance, in which you are jointly concerned with the Church-wardens, is the keeping of the Regifter Book. The 70th Canon directs, that it be of Parchment: and though an Act of Parliament, lately paffed, allows Marriages to be regiftered in a Paper Book; yet Parchment is far more durable: nor is the Difference of Expence worth regarding, as it returns fo feldom. This Book fhould be ftrongly bound, and not over large; left it fhould be worn and damaged, before it is filled. For the fafe Prefervation of it, and doubtlefs of all preceding Books of the fame Kind, the Canon orders, that a Cheft be provided with three Locks and Keys; one for you, one for each of the Church-wardens, who are ordinarily two; and that on Sundays, if there hath been any Chriftening, Marriage or Burial, in the Week before, it fhall be entered there. I am afraid it is feldom thus kept: and yet there would be no great trouble in it, after a little Ufe. Or where that is otherwife, either the Minifter or a Church-warden fhould keep it: and each of them fhould fee from Time to Time, how

it

it is kept. The Entries, if they cannot well be made every Sunday, should be made very frequently, and in the mean Time the Minister, if he hath not the Book, should take Memorandums. He is the Person directed to write in it, and usually much the fittest. But if, through any Accident that happens not to be so, he should appoint a proper Person, and superintend him. The Names and Surnames of the Parents ought to be added, in registering not only Baptisms, where it is enjoined, but Marriages and Burials too, as far as may be: for it may prevent Doubts and Disputes. It will also be very useful, to put down the Day of the Birth and Death of each Person, as well as of the Baptism and Burial. The late Act above-mentioned hath directed farther, that every Page of the Register of Marriages be numbered, to discover if any Leaf be afterwards cut out: and ruled with Lines at equal Distances, to discover if any Article be afterwards put in. And you will do very well to observe the same Precautions in registering Baptisms and Burials. When a Page is filled, the Canon requires the Minister and Church-

fifth Charge to his CLERGY.

Church-wardens to subscribe their Names; which they should do just below the last Line. And if this be not done immediately, it may without any Inconvenience be done soon after: and was done by me and the Church-wardens, for many Years, in one of the most populous Parishes of the Kingdom. Lastly the Canon requires, that an attested Copy of this Book be annually transmitted to the Bishop's Registry, received without Fee, and faithfully preserved there: and it authorizes me to proceed against those, who are negligent about any of its Directions. I must therefore both intreat and insist, that you inquire in what Condition your old and your present Register Books are, and get them kept for the future as they ought. I have more than once been put under great Difficulties in Ordinations, for Want of Exactness in the Register of Baptisms. That of Marriages is of so great Concern, that altering it designedly to establish or void a Marriage is by the Act above-mentioned made Felony. In all Cases the Book, faithfully kept, is good Evidence: and falsifying it, is punishable at common Law. I would only observe

observe farther on this Head, that in the Preamble of a Bill, which passed the House of Commons this last Session, and had a second Reading in the House of Lords, it was asserted as notorious, that " great In-
" conveniences have arisen from the present
" defective Manner, in which parochial Re-
" gisters are formed, and the loose and un-
" certain Method, in which they are kept
" and preserved; whereby the Evidence of
" Descents is frequently lost and rendered
" precarious." So far as this may be Fact it will be most for our Honour to amend it, without the Interposition of the Legislature.

A fourth Point, of which I hope you will think yourselves bound, if not by Law, yet in Conscience, to take a joint Care with the Church-wardens, is that of parochial Charities. The Minister is the Representative of the Church, intrusted with its Interests; and you ought to endeavour, that such Benefactions be first preserved and then applied in a proper Manner.

If it be doubtful, whether such or such a Donation hath been given to your Church or
Poor,

Poor, or the Support of a School in your Parish, you will make proper Inquiry concerning the Matter. If it be given by any Writing, you will procure that Writing, or an attested Copy of it, to be laid up safely, either in the Parish Chest, or the Bishop's Registry; indeed a Copy in each Place would be best; and an Account of the Gift should be inserted in your Parish Book. For if Deeds are left in private Hands, and especially without authentic Notice where they are left, they are sometimes designedly suppressed; and often undesignedly destroyed or lost, through the Ignorance or Carelessness of the Persons possessed of them. It will also be very proper, to have a Table mentioning the Charity, hung up in your Church, that a grateful Remembrance of the Benefactors may be continued to Posterity, and others incited to follow their good Example: as a Paper of Directions drawn up by the Lower House of Convocation in 1710, hath well expressed it[k]. If the Benefaction be an Estate vested in Trustees, it will be very material to get the Trust renewed in due Time;

[k] See *Wilkins*, Vol. iv. P. 638.

Time; else in all Likelihood there will be Expence; if not Danger; and to Trustees of as good Credit and Ability, as possible. They must likewise be warned, never to let out such Lands in long Leases, or at very low Rents, in Favour of any Body: but to raise the Rents when they can; at least to vary them, which will make it easy to raise them, when there is Opportunity: otherwise it will soon be pretended, that they have no Right to raise them; of which there are some unhappy Instances in this Diocese. If the Gift be in Money, you must press to have it placed in the public Funds, in Case it be considerable enough; or else in the best private Hands, and on the best Security that can be obtained: paying no Regard in such Cases to personal Friendships; and being particularly careful that Parish Officers do not keep it in their own Custody. If they do, the Interest will usually be paid out of the public Money, and most probably the Principal will be lost in a few Years.

But Charities are preserved in vain, unless they are well applied; and they are often sadly

sadly misapplied. Gifts to the Church, where it is not otherwise expressed, must be supposed intended for beautifying the Church: else it will be never the better for such Gifts: for it will be equally repaired without them: the Parishioners are bound to that: and the Chief of the Burden usually falls upon the richest, for whose Relief Charities were certainly not intended. And yet such Benefactions are too commonly employed, not only in mere Repairs, but in what hath no Connection with the Fabric; in providing Bread and Wine for the Communion, in paying Church-wardens Bills for all Sorts of Things, it may be for extravagant and riotous Entertainments amongst the rest, in easing the Poors Rates, in I know not what; and the Church all the Time, instead of being any Way improved, suffered to grow dirty and even ruinous. A lamentable Abuse of this Kind, (where a Steeple fell down, and was in Part rebuilt by Contribution, while an Estate, more than sufficient to have kept the whole Building in good Order and Beauty, was perverted to other Uses) I have taken much Pains to rectify, but fear it is not thoroughly rectified yet. Again, Gifts to the Poor were certainly intended for the Benefit of the Poor; to make Provision for such of them as are not on the Parish List, or a better Provision for such as are. And yet they are sometimes embezzled and squandered, in a great Measure, if not wholly; sometimes bestowed to serve private or Party Purposes: and very frequently sunk into the legal Rate; so the Wealthy are benefited; and the Needy have not a Farthing more, than if Nothing had been given for them.

I know it is not always easy, perhaps not always possible for you, to remedy these ill Practices. But a reat Part of the Blame will be laid on you, right or wrong, unless you try to remedy them. And it may prove less difficult than you imagine. Church-wardens and Overseers perhaps are ignorant, or going on thoughtlessly, and would be thankful to you for good Advice: or however would be ruled by it, on your representing to them the Heinousness of robbing God or the Poor; and the Honour it will do them, and the Consolation it will afford them, to

have

have put Things into a right Channel. Or supposing them backward to comply, you may be able to get considerable Persons in the Parish or Neighbourhood to second you. At least you will get the Reputation of a most laudable Zeal, and if you conduct that Zeal aright, of Discretion also: and these together may produce unexpected Success; especially where the Abuse is not yet become inveterate. But if Nothing else will do, and the Case be plain, and the Object of sufficient Importance: Recourse should be had to the Authority of the Law: and you should be willing to bear a Proportion of the Charges, if it be requisite and you are able; only taking the strictest Care to proceed with Mildness and Fairness.

I have now finished the Course of Directions to you, which I began 15 Years ago. And as I can truly say, that in this and every Part of my Behaviour as your Bishop, I have, through the Divine Assistance, diligently laboured to do my Duty with Uprightness, and promote your Good and that of your Parishioners, present and future; so I hope you will accept my Endeavours with Candour

Candour and Study to profit by them; excusing my Failings, which I know have been many, and will now be too likely to increase. I am advancing apace into the Decline of Age. Three of my Brethren[1], my oldest and best Friends, have gone before me in less than twelve Months. I must expect to follow them soon. Whether I may live, or, if I live, whether I may be able, to meet you thus again, God only can foresee. May he grant us to meet in a better World!

But before I conclude, permit me to subjoin to these general Admonitions, a few Words concerning two particular Occurrences.

In the first Place I return you my hearty Thanks for the Pains, which you have taken in Behalf of the Society for propagating the Gospel. The Collection hath upon the Whole been made very successfully throughout the Kingdom; and amounts to almost 19,000*l.* if not more: whereas ten Years ago it fell short of 15,000*l.* But I believe the Contribution of this County hath been in Proportion the largest of any. The last Time it was

---

[1] Bishops *Butler*, *Benson*, and *Berkley*.

barely

barely 300*l.* nor was that to be accounted small: and now it is very near 500*l.* I mean in both Cases exclusive of the University: which distinguished itself very honourably then, and I doubt not, will at present. May God increase, and bless, and reward the Zeal of all his Servants every where for supporting, and enlarging the Kingdom of his Son, and making the Confession of his Name effectual to the Salvation of Mankind.

The other Subject, on which I would speak to you, is the Contest about Representatives for this County in the next Parliament. Let no one be alarmed. I need not, and I do not mean, to give you at a Meeting of this Nature, my Opinion which of the Candidates you ought to prefer: of that I say no more here than that you ought to regard, in the first Place, the inseparable Interests of the excellent Church we are Members of, and, its only human Support, the just and gracious Government we live under; then other subordinate Considerations. My Purpose is merely to exhort you, *(and I beseech you, Brethren, suffer the Word of Exhortation* ᵐ) *that on this Occasion, your Converſation be ſuch as becometh the Goſpel of Chriſt:* in doing which, I have neither one Party, nor one Perſon amongſt you, more in my View than another: but if I may uſe the Apoſtle's Words, *am jealous with a godly Jealouſy over you all* ⁿ. I cannot indeed ſuppoſe, that any of you would be guilty of the groſſer Faults too common at ſuch Times, or any wilful wrong Behaviour. But in the Midſt of ſo many Claſhings, Provocations, and Diſappointments, as will happen, ſo many Miſtakes and Miſrepreſentations as ariſe one knows not how: the Incitements to uncharitable and contemptuous Thoughts, to unadviſed and injurious Words, in Anger or in Mirth, nay to unkind and hard and even unjuſt Actions, are very great, and the beſt of us all ſhould be continually ſuggeſting to our Minds proper Cautions for avoiding theſe Dangers. Elſe we ſhall fall into Sin againſt God and our Neighbour: we ſhall loſe the Eſteem of Part of thoſe whoſe Improvement by us depends on their eſteeming us; and ſet a bad inſtead of a good Example to the Reſt.

ᵐ Heb xiii. 22.   ⁿ 2 Cor. xi. 2.

Let every one of us therefore be very watchful over our Conduct: or if we have not been so, let us amend it: and if we find preserving our Innocence difficult, let us meddle the less with these Matters: for indeed being over busy about them is not very suitable to our Function. But while we are strict with ourselves, let us be very mild in Regard to others, whom we think to have done amiss: we may blame them without Cause; or if we do not, it is easy to err; and we, amongst others, are sadly liable to Faults. But let us be especially mild towards our own Brethren. For why should we diminish our little remaining Strength by intestine Dissentions, and teach yet more Persons to think ill or meanly of us, than do already? Surely the common Cause of Religion and Virtue, which we are jointly intrusted to support, should have infinitely greater Force to unite us, than any Thing else to divide us.

Next to yourselves, you will study to preserve as many of your Parishioners as possible, from the Sins *that so easily beset them* at these Seasons of epidemical Unreasonableness and Licentiousness. Those, who are of your own

own Side, you may counsel and reprove more freely. With the rest you must be extremely calm and patient: take the most favourable Opportunities, and use the most persuasive Methods of speaking: but in some Way or other, private or public, all, who need it, should be told, *whether they will bear or whether they will forbear,* that the great Christian Laws of Dutifulness to Superiors, mutual Good-will, Forbearance, Forgiveness, Equity, Veracity, Moderation, Sobriety, lose not the least of their Obligation during the Continuance of these Disputes: that all Virtues are to be chiefly exercised, when they are chiefly tried: and that therefore now more particularly, you, as the Apostle directs, must *put them in Mind,* and they must keep in Mind, *to be subject to Principalities and Powers, to obey Magistrates, to be ready to every good Work, to speak Evil of no Man, to be no Brawler but gentle, shewing all Meekness unto all Men*°. I end this long Discourse in the Words of the same Apostle: *Finally, Brethren, whatsoever Things are true, whatsoever Things are venerable,* (for so the Word is rightly transla-

° Tit. iii. 1, 2.

ted

ted in the Margin) *whatsoever Things are just whatsoever Things are pure, whatsoever Things are lovely, whatsoever Things are of good Report, if there be any Virtue and if there be any Praise, think of* and do *these Things: and the God of Peace shall be with you* [p].

[p] Phil. iv. 8, 9.

A CHARGE

A

CHARGE

DELIVERED TO THE

CLERGY of the DIOCESE

OF

CANTERBURY,

In the YEAR 1758.

Reverend Brethren,

THE Difpofer of all Things having permitted his Majefty, by the Advice of his faithful Servants, to nominate me for your Bifhop: though I faw many Reafons to dread this Promotion, arifing from the Difficulties of the Office and of the Times, from the great Qualities of my Predeceffors, and my own increafing Weakneffes; yet I thought myfelf bound to obey his Commands, and with the fame Gratitude for his favourable Opinion, as if I had wifhed to receive them: determining, through God's Grace, to perform the Duties of my Station as well as I could; and hoping for the Candor, the Affiftance, and the Prayers of good People. To make fome Amends by Diligence for my Deficiencies in other Refpects, I refolved immediately to vifit my Diocefe: for which Purpofe we are here affembled.

Thefe

These Meetings were designed, partly to give the Clergy Opportunities of conferring with each other, and consulting their Superiors, on Matters relating to their Profession; and I am very desirous, that you should render them as beneficial in this Way, as possible: but principally, to give Bishops Opportunities of exhorting and cautioning their Clergy, either on such general Subjects as are always useful, or on such particular Occasions as the Circumstances of Things, or the Inquiries, made at or against these Times, point out; and of interposing their Authority, if there be Need; which amongst you, I am persuaded, there will not. To provide more fully for your Instruction, I have ordered a Charge to be sent you, which I delivered to the Clergy of *Oxfordshire*, and printed at their Request, about twenty Years ago. Would to God it were become unseasonable now. But, as unhappily it is not, I earnestly recommend the Contents of it to your most serious Thoughts: and would have you look on what I shall at present say further, as supplemental to it.

Counsels and Admonitions to parochial Ministers pre-suppose their Residence. The Founders of Parishes provided them with Glebes, and built Houses for them, purposely that they might reside. The Laws of the Church have from the Beginning, and do still require, as indeed common Equity doth, that this valuable Consideration, for which these Endowments were given, should be faithfully paid. And going over and performing the Service from Time to Time, or engaging some other Clergyman to take Care of it, or of the occasional Part of it, seldom answers the original Intention. Your People will not so readily, and cannot so conveniently, apply to the Minister of another Parish: And when they do, his Assistance, for the most Part, will be less early, or less constant, than it should: though doubtless they, who have undertaken to supply their Neighbours Absence, ought to do it very conscientiously. But besides, even the Sunday-Duty, when the Incumbent unnecessarily comes from a distant Place to do it, will be considered as accompanied with something like a Breach of the Sunday, will not always

always be kept to the stated Hours, will often be hurried over indecently: the Catechism will either not be taught or not expounded, if the Distance be at all considerable; nor probably will the Sermon be well adapted to the Audience. For it is only living amongst your people, and knowing them thoroughly that can shew you, what is level to their Capacities, and suited to their Circumstances; what will reform their Faults, and improve their Hearts in true Goodness. Yet this is your Business with them: and unless you perform it, every Thing else is Nothing. Further, such as want your Help most may not come to your Sermons, or may not apply them to their own Case, or may need to have them enforced by Considerations peculiar to themselves, and unfit to be specified in Public. Speaking to them separately, and agreeably to their several States of Mind and Life, may have unforeseen Influence. And being always at Hand, to order the disorderly, and countenance the well-behaved, to advise and comfort the diseased and afflicted, to relieve or procure Relief for the necessitous, to compose

pose little Differences and discourage wrong Customs in the Beginning, to promote friendly Offices, and keep up an edifying and entertaining Conversation in a Neighbourhood, must add incredible Weight to public Instruction.

Indeed your Congregations expect these Things from you, and have a Right to expect them. The Nature of your Office requires them: you have all at your Ordination expressly promised to *use both public and private Monitions and Exhortations, both to the sick and whole within your Cures, as Need shall require and Occasion be given, the Lord being your Helper.* Now we cannot use them duly, without being resident. But further still, since their Ordination, all Vicars have sworn particularly to be resident unless they are dispensed with, which means by lawful Authority: nor doth any Dispensation of a Bishop last beyond his own Time; or beyond the Term for which he gave it; or, if that were indefinite, beyond his Pleasure: Points, which Vicars ought to consider much more seriously, than they often do. And every Rector

Rector hath sworn in general to *obey* his Bishop *in all Things lawful and honest*. Now surely Residence is lawful and honest: and what is punishable by a Bishop may, if done without his Leave, be well interpreted Disobedience to him: and the Non-residence of Rectors is punishable just in the same Manner with that of Vicars.

It must not therefore be pleaded, that however necessary the Residence of some Minister may be, that of a Curate may suffice. For your Engagement is, not merely that the several Duties of your Parish shall be done, but that you personally will do them: and if it were enough to substitute another to do them, a Layman would be, in Point of Reason and Conscience, as capable of holding a Benefice, as a Man in holy Orders. Besides, a Curate will usually have less Knowledge and less Experience, than the Incumbent: and he and the Parishioners will conceive, that they are less related to each other. He will consider himself, as being with them only for an uncertain, and he may hope, a short Time; which will tempt him to neglect

lect them. And they will consider him, as not the Person, who hath Authority over them; which will tempt them to disregard him: especially as the largest Salary, that can be legally appointed, or generally afforded to a Curate, will not enable him to recommend himself to them by doing Good amongst them in any expensive Way: whilst yet the people will think, and justly too, that the whole Income of the Benefice was intended to procure them a Minister, to do them as much Good in every Way, as could reasonably be expected from it.

There are indeed Cases, in which the Law dispenses with holding two Livings, and by Consequence allows absence from one. But Persons ought to consider well: supposing they can with Innocence take the Benefit of that Law; whether they can do it on other Terms, than their Dispensation and their Bond expresses, of preaching yearly thirteen Sermons, and keeping two Months Hospitality, in the Parish where they reside least. For the leave given them on these Conditions, is not intended to be given them, however legally valid, if the Conditions are neglected:

neglected: always excepting where juft Impediments happen. There are likewife Cafes, in which the Non-refidence of Perfons, who have only one Living, is permitted by Law. But fome of thefe alfo are put under Limitations, beyond which the Permiffion doth not reach.

Further ftill, I am fenfible, that Confiderations of Health and ftrength, and particular Circumftances of Incumbents or their Families, require Leave of Abfence to be fometimes allowed, where the Law makes no Allowance. But then it fhould never be taken for any confiderable Time, without being afked: nor fhould it be afked without good Caufe. And mere Fancy, or Defire of living more at eafe, or in a cheerfuller, and, it may be, lefs clerical Manner, is by no means a fufficient Caufe. Nor indeed is the Allegation of Health to be urged too far, or to be too much regarded. For Places, called unwholefome, prove upon Trial very wholefome to many Perfons: and thofe, which are leaft fo, muft have fome Minifters in or near them; and whom rather, generally fpeaking, than fuch as enjoy the whole Profits? Much lefs is In-

dulgence

dulgence to be granted for every present Convenience, or Prospect of temporal Advantage: which if Clergymen appear to have greatly at heart, and the care of their Parishes but little, indeed it looks very ill.

Another Plea may be offered by some, that though they live not on their own Cures, they serve others. And it is not always an insufficient one. But, with very few Exceptions, the most natural and most useful Method by far is, that each take the Oversight of the Parish, which properly belongs to him: and absenting himself from that, for a little more Income, a little more Agreeableness, or any slight Reason, is unbecoming and unwarrantable Behaviour.

At the same Time I acknowledge, that the Poorness of some Benefices makes the Residence of a distinct Minister upon each of them impracticable: and therefore they must be served from an adjoining Parish, or a greater Distance; and no more Duty expected, than there is a competent Provision for. But then I fear, indeed I have found, that in some Benefices, not so poor, one Minister supplies two Churches on a Sunday; contrary to a repeated Injunction of succeſſive Archbiſhops to their Suffragans, which they certainly deſigned to obſerve themſelves; and the Words of which are theſe; *that you do not allow any Miniſter to ſerve more than one Church or Chapel in one Day, except that Chapel be a Member of the Pariſh Church; or united thereunto; and unleſs the ſaid Church or Chapel be not able to maintain a Curate.* The Conſequence of diſregarding this Injunction is, not only the very bad one, that the Service is performed in irreverent Haſte, but that Catechiſing is neglected in both Places, if not altogether, yet in a great Degree. Nay, perhaps for great Part of the Year, if not the Whole, each of them hath Prayers but once. Where indeed it can be truly alledged in this laſt caſe, that the Inhabitants of each Pariſh not only with Convenience may, but actually do attend at both Churches, the Plea muſt be allowed its Weight. But, as to other Excuſes: If the Number of the People be ſmall, the ſervice is not leſs enjoined, and is more eaſily performed: If they had rather have a Sermon at another Church, than merely Prayers at their own; they ought to have

more

more than Prayers; an Expofition of the Catechifm, which they will account equivalent to a Sermon: or you may reduce it with eafe into the Form of a Sermon: and then many of them will come to their own Church, who now go to no other, but profane the reft of the Day: if they are content with Part of the Sunday Service, which however may be faid or believed without fufficient Ground, yet probably they would be glad of the Whole. But fuppofing them to be indifferent about it, or even averfe from it, their Minifter is bound to fhew them, that they ought not. And how long foever this hath been the Practice; if it ought not to have been fo at all, the longer the worfe. My pious and learned Predeceffor, Archbifhop *Potter*, lamented heavily to me the Irregularities of this Kind, which he found in this Diocefe: and if any remain, I muft, after his Example, endeavour to have them rectified.

I hope they will be rectified by the beft Method, beyond Comparifon; your own ferious Reflections on what you owe to your Flocks, and what you owe to the great Shepherd of Souls. Though you are ever fo expresly permitted by human Laws to be absent from your Cures, or by your Ordinary to serve them, or let them be served, by Halves; you are answerable to an infinitely higher Tribunal for what God, and not Man alone, hath made your duty. Therefore, if you regard the Peace of your own Souls and your final Comfort, you will never do any of these Things, unless very strong Reasons oblige yon to it: and you will never be glad of such Reasons, but heartily sorry. You will give your Parishes both Morning and Evening Prayer, wherever it is possible: and you will supply them in Person, unless particular Circumstances render it impracticable, or unless, by living at a distance for the present, you are more useful to Religion some other Way, and peculiarly qualified for that Usefulness. Far from catching at weak Pretences, you will rather be diffident about strong Inducements: and much readier to follow the Directions, than solicit the Indulgence of your Superiors. But if any do chuse the worse Part, they must remember, that we Bishops are bound to oppose, instead of consulting their Inclinations, from Concern

for

for them, as well as their Parishioner. And therefore you will not ... it real ... nature to connive ... of this kind presumptuously taken without leave, or to grant Requests made for them, as Matters of Course: nor impute it to a Fondness of **exercising** Power when Compliance with the **Rules of** the Church is required: nor yet hastily condemn it, as partial Behaviour, if an Indulgence, denied to one, is granted to another; for there may be, in the Cases of different Persons, considerable Disparities, unknown to you, or unobserved by you.

But when it is ever so clear, that the Non-residence of Ministers ought to be allowed, it is at least equally clear, that they should use their best Endeavours to make their People Amends for it. One Thing, proper to be done for this End, is relieving their Poor: which as they could not with Decency avoid doing, according to their Ability, if they lived amongst them, they ought to do more largely, if they live elsewhere. For no Reproach will lie heavier on our Order, than that of reaping all, and sowing nothing: whereas, they who give Alms in their Absence,

fence, will be in Effect always present to one valuable Purpose; will be readily presumed to be Well-wishers to their Parishes in every way; whilst they are Benefactors to them in this Way: and by such a Specimen of the Influence of Religion upon themselves will remind their Congregations, very acceptably, of the Influence, which it ought to have upon them; especially if they make their Charity more directly subservient to Religion, by affording distinguished Encouragement to pious and virtuous Persons, and those who appear likely to be made such: by procuring Children to be instructed in their Christian Duty, and other proper Knowledge; by distributing useful Books amongst the needy and ignorant. What is thus bestowed, is of all the Service it can be: whereas injudicious Bounty may even produce Harm.

Another Thing, incumbent on such as cannot reside constantly, is to inspect however the State of their Parishes as frequently as they can: spending Days, or Weeks, or longer Seasons there occasionally; and in Proportion as their Time is shorter, using more Diligence in public and private Instructions

structions and Warnings. For they are peculiarly bound to do what they are able, who are not able to do what else they ought. But if even this be out of their Power, they may at least be assiduous in getting Informations from Persons of Understanding and Seriousness, in or near their Cures, with what Regularity, with what Spirit and Zeal, each Part of the Parochial Duty is performed; whether true inward Piety makes any Progress; whether any and what Abuses and Neglects are crept in. And he who reckons it enough, that for ought he knows to the contrary, his Parishioners go on like their Neighbours, hath by no Means the requisite Concern for their Souls, or his own.

But whenever Absence is necessary, or the Largeness of a Parish, or the Infirmity of a Minister, hinders him from taking the whole Care of it personally, the principal Point is the Choice of a fit Substitute, to be employed in his Stead, or share his Burthen: for no Superintendency will make an unfit one answer the End. And therefore I charge it upon your Consciences, not to suffer Cheapness, Recommendation of Friends, Affection to this or that Person or Place of Education, in short, any Inducement whatever to weigh near so much with you, as the Benefit of your People, in chusing Persons to serve your Churches. For on you the Choice of them lies in the first Place: but not on you alone. The Laws of the Church require, particularly Can. 48, that *no Curate or Minister be permitted to serve in any Place, without Examination and Admission of the Ordinary:* in Consequence of which, one of the beforementioned archiepiscopal Directions to the Suffragans of the Province, is this: *That you make diligent Inquiry concerning Curates in your Diocese; and proceed to ecclesiastical Censures against those, who shall presume to serve Cures, without being first duly licensed thereunto; as also against all Incumbents, who shall receive and employ them without obtaining such Licence.* Yet I would avoid Rigour in all Cases. The Expence of a Licence, by Means of the Stamps, may to some be rather inconvenient, and greater than the Government perhaps intended: at least, if they are likely to remove, and so repeat that Expence, in a short time. And such Curates I would

would excuse: only desiring them to consider, what Security of continuing in their Station, and receiving their Salary, a Licence brings them. But then you cannot think it right, that I should be left in Ignorance, who serves a Church under my Care, till I learn it by Accident, or private Inquiry, perhaps many Months after; through which Omission, Men of bad Characters, Men not in Orders, may intrude; as there hath lately been a flagrant Instance in this Diocese. I am far from looking on the past Failures of giving Notice, as designed Negligence of your Flocks, or Disrespect to your Superiors. But I shall have Cause both to think of them and treat them as such, if continued after the Warning, which I now give, that no one is to officiate statedly, or employ another to officiate so, within my Jurisdiction, unless he first obtain my Consent; or what in Effect will be mine, that of your very worthy and vigilant Archdeacon. Think not, I beg you, that this is taking more on myself, than my Predecessors did. Their own Directions prove, that they would have done the same Thing, if they had seen the same Necessity,

Necessity. Far be it from me to *lord it over God's Heritage*[a]: but I am bound to *keep that which is committed to my Trust*[b].

When you want Curates, I recommend it to you, first to enquire after Persons of Merit, already ordained, and if possible ordained Priests, taking Care to see their Orders, as well as to examine into their Characters, before you think of granting Nominations to others. The Number of Clergymen indeed is rather deficient, than superfluous. But still one would not add to it by overlooking undeservedly those who are of it already. And particularly where help is wanted only for a short Time, I shall insist on this Point: nor will, without absolute Necessity, ordain any one upon such a Title. And if fraudulent Titles are brought, merely to procure Orders, as I hope I shall discover them soon enough to disallow them, so I shall be sure to remark and remember, who hath attempted to impose upon me by them.

The next Thing to be considered in Relation to Curates is, their Testimonials. And here the Canon and Directions already quoted

[a] 1 Pet. v. 3. [b] 1 Tim. vi. 20.

enjoin,

enjoin, that no Bishop *admit such as remove out of another Diocese to serve in his, without the Testimony in Writing of the Bishop of that Diocese, or Ordinary of the peculiar Jurisdiction, from whence they come, of their good Life, Ability, and Conformity to the ecclesiastical Laws of the Church of England.* For the Clergymen of one Diocese, or Jurisdiction, at least their Hand-writing, being usually unknown to the Bishop of another, he can seldom, of himself, be sure, either that he hath their genuine Testimony, or how far he may trust it. Therefore it is fit, that he should desire the Attestation of their proper Superior. And even to this it will be prudent to add such further Information, as can be got: considering how very carelessly Testimonials are sometimes granted, even by reputable Persons.

But let me intreat you never to be guilty of such Carelessness yourselves, for whatever Purpose one is asked of you. Both the Nature of the Thing, and the Directions repeatedly mentioned, require, that no Bishop accept any Letters Testimonial, *unless it be declared by those who shall sign them, that they*

have

have *personally known*, not only the Man, but his *Life and Conversation, for the Time by them certified*; and do believe in their Conscience, that he is qualified *for that Order, Office or Employment, which he desires*. Now Testimonials concerning such Things as these, cannot be Matter of mere Form, unless our whole Profession be a very empty Form. We, the Bishops to whom they are given, do not, and must not, understand them to be so: it would be absurd to demand them if we did. Some Customs indeed may grow to be Things of Course: the Reasons for them ceasing, or not being thought of Moment; and yet the Law for them continuing. But the Reasons for Testimonials can never cease or be thought of small Moment. They are the only ordinary Information that we have, in a Case of the utmost Importance, in which we have a Right to be informed. For no one can imagine, that we are to ordain and employ whoever comes, or depend on clandestine Intelligence. We must therefore and to depend on regular Testimonials. And if they be untrue, we are most injuriously deceived by them: and all the Mischiefs, that follow from thence, will sit heavy one Day on the Deceivers. But, even exclusively of this great Consideration, would you be chargeable with declaring a deliberate Falsehood under your Hand? Would you have unworthy Men fill ecclesiastical Stations and exclude their Betters? Would you have your Bishop reproached, and your Order vilified, through your Fault? If not; remember, how utterly inconsistent with all Concern for Religion, with all Veracity, Probity and Prudence it is, to sign Testimonials at random; how lamentable a Sort of Clergy it will produce; how dreadful an Encouragement to Wickedness and Profaneness it will prove. Remember also, that you express in these Instruments, not what you charitably hope a Person will be; but what you actually know he hath been: not what others tell you at the End of the Time, for which you vouch; but what you have seen and heard through the Course of it: so that, if for a considerable Part of the three Years, commonly specified, you have seen and heard Nothing of him, for that Part you can certify Nothing about him. And remember,

lastly,

laftly, that though the Affirmation of a Perfon's having lived pioufly, foberly and honeftly, comprehends a great deal, yet the concluding Article, your Belief of his Fitnefs for what he defires, implies a great deal more. For let him be ever fo good and even learned a Man, he cannot be fit for a Clergyman and the Care of a Parifh, without competent Gravity and Difcretion, and a Voice and a Manner fuitable to a public Affembly: of all which Things they, that have had fome Familiarity with him, are ufually the beft, if not the only Judges. This Part of the Teftimonial therefore is highly neceffary: and every Part of it muft be well confidered, before it is given; and no Regard paid to Neighbourhood, Acquaintance, Friendfhip, Compaffion, Importunity, when they ftand in Competition with Truth.

It may fometimes be hard for you to refufe your Hand to improper Perfons. But it is only one of the many Hardfhips, which Confcience bids Men undergo refolutely, when they are called to them. It would be much harder, that your Bifhop fhould be mifled, the Church of God injured, and the poor Wretch himself affisted to invade sacrilegiously an Office, at the Thought of which he hath Cause to tremble. And if you fear he will be revenged on you for not yielding to him, this furnishes an additional Reason for denying him: for will you, or can you, say of such a one, that he is qualified to be a Minister of the Gospel any where? But if the Persons, to whom Candidates apply, would only make it a Rule to meet, and act jointly on the Occasion, and keep secret the Particulars of what passed, it might be unknown, from whom the Denial proceeded. Or suppose it known, the Resentment of such, as deserve to be refused, will seldom do a worthy Man much Hurt: and a Number of such Refusals will do the Public unspeakable Good. Indeed the Expectation of a Refusal's following upon wrong Behaviour will in a great Degree prevent such Behaviour, and turn this whole Difficulty into a Pleasure. But what is unavoidable with Innocence, must be virtuously born: and instead of submitting to recommend unfit Persons, you ought, if others recommend them, which God forbid, to interpose immediate Cautions against the Danger, in all flagrant Cases. Still not every past Fault, nor every present Infirmity, should be alledged, or allowed, as an Impediment. But into an Office, the most important of all others, none should be admitted, who are void of the proper Spirit, or a competent Share of the needful Qualifications for it: and the less, because, though we can refuse to ordain them, we often cannot keep them back from very unsuitable Stations, when once they are ordained.

After presenting the Title and Testimonials, whether for Orders, a Curacy, or a Living, follows the Examination. For though the Testimonial expresses an Opinion that the Person is qualified; which may be very useful, to restrain such from applying as are notoriously unqualified; yet we Bishops must not, especially in the Case of Orders, rest on a mere Opinion; but assure ourselves by a closer Trial, whether he hath sufficient Knowledge of Religion and the Holy Scriptures to teach them in public, and apply them

them in private, and defend them againſt Oppoſers: the two firſt of which are abſolutely neceſſary; the third, highly requiſite. As therefore, on the one Hand, I hope I never have been or ſhall be over ſtrict in this Reſpect, and rejecting Candidates will give me, almoſt, if not quite, as much Concern, as it can give them: ſo on the other, I muſt adhere to my Duty; againſt all Solicitations of Friends, and all Intreaties of the Parties concerned, who little think what they do, when they preſs into ſuch an Employment prematurely. I ſhew my Regard to you, when I exclude unqualified Perſons out of your Number: and I ſhall never doubt your candid Interpretation of my Conduct; nor indeed your Zeal to vindicate it, when you are acquainted with my Reaſons, which any of you ſhall, who hath Cauſe to aſk them. But that no Injuſtice may be done to thoſe whom I poſtpone, any more than to myſelf: I beſeech you to conſider, and, if needful, to ſay in their Behalf, that though deficient in Knowledge, they may have a Goodneſs of Heart, more valuable than the higheſt Knowledge: though not qualified yet, they may be foon; may already have made a good Progress, though not a sufficient one; may indeed have more Learning on the Whole, than many who are admitted, only not have applied themselves enough to theological Learning.

Examination must occasionally be repeated after Persons have been ordained. The 39th Canon requires it before Institution to Benefices: therefore surely it is advisable also before Admission to Curacies. A Man, who was fit to be ordained, may have become since, through Negligence, or bodily Indisposition affecting his Mind, unfit to be employed: or he may be capable still of what he was ordained for, but not of what he applies for: or his Ordainer, though ever so duly careful, may sometimes have mistaken, or been misinformed: and if he hath chanced to be too indulgent, the bad Effects of his Indulgence ought to be prevented. Accordingly Re-examination is common. My Brethren the Bishops, I am sure, will not blame me for using it: and I trust, you my Brethren will not.

When

When a Curate nominated hath been examined and approved, the next Step is, to appoint him a Salary. And here I am very sensible, that what is far from a comfortable Maintenance for Life, may however be a tolerable Competency at first: and likewise, that some Benefices are so mean, and some Incumbents in such low Circumstances, or burthened with so numerous Families, that they must be excused, if they endeavour to get Help on as easy Terms, as they well can. But if any Minister, who hath either a large Preferment, or two moderate ones, or a plentiful temporal Income, tries to make a hard Bargain with his Brother, whom he employs; and is more solicitous to give the smallest Salary possible, than to find the worthiest Person; it is Matter of severe and just Reproach: the Friends of the Clergy will be scandalized at it: their Enemies will take dreadful Advantages of it: indeed the People in general, if we think a Trifle enough for him that doth the Work, will be apt to conceive it very needless, that he, who doth little or nothing, should have a great deal more. For this Reason therefore,

P 4   amongst

amongſt imcomparably weightier ones, it concerns you much, both to labour diligently, and to allow liberally. Accordingly I hope I ſhall never have the diſagreeable Office thrown upon me of augmenting what is propoſed, but the Satisfaction given me of confirming and applauding it.

But beſides making a reaſonable Allowance, the Miniſter of a Pariſh ought to provide, with the kindeſt Attention in all Reſpects, for the Convenience and Accommodation, the Credit and Influence, of his Curate: who is bound in Return to conſult faithfully the Miniſter's Honour and Intereſt in every thing; but above all, to be unwearied in that beſt Proof of his Gratitude, a conſcientious Care of the Souls committed to him; not proportioning his Diligence to the poor Recompence paid him here, but to the unſpeakable Happineſs reſerved for good Shepherds hereafter.

Indeed whether the Principal, or his Repreſentative, or both reſide, their Induſtry and Fervency and Prudence will be the Meaſure of their people's Benefit, and their own final Acceptance. If you content yourſelves

selves with a languid formal Recital of stated Offices, and by Indolence, or Amusements, or Business, or even Studies, are lost to your Parishioners, while you are in the Midst of them, or by Indiscretions in Conversation, Dress, or Demeanour, become disliked or despised by them, you may in Respect of any spiritual Usefulness to them or yourselves, be, almost as well, perhaps better, ever so far off. But this is no Excuse for being absent, but only a Reason for being present to good Purpose. And as the Non-residence of some, the unactive Residence of others, and the offensive Conduct of a third Sort, (which cause great Sorrow, but moderate Complaints amongst wise and good People,) are favourite Topics of Invective against us, not only in the Mouths of irreligious Persons, but of a new Sect pretending to the strictest Piety; though we are bound always, we are peculiarly bound at present, to behave in so exemplary a Manner, as will *cut off Occasion from them which desire Occasion to glory*[c] of themselves, and speak Evil of us. It is not *rendering* to

[c] 2 Cor. xi. 12.

them *Railing for Railing* [d]; it is not ridiculing them, especially in Terms bordering on Profaneness, or affecting more gravely to hold them in Contempt; it is not doing them the Honour of miscalling other Persons of more than ordinary Seriousness by their Name, that will prevent the Continuance or the Increase of the Harm, which they are doing. The only Way is, for the Clergy to imitate and emulate what is good in them, avoiding what is bad: to attend their Cures, edify their Parishioners with awakening, but rational and scriptural, Discourses, converse much with them as *Watchmen for their Souls* [e], *be sober, grave, temperate, and shew themselves in all Things Patterns of good Works* [f]. If the People see, or but imagine, their Minister unwilling to take more Pains about them, or preserve more Guard upon himself than for Shame he must, no Wonder if it alienates them powerfully both from him and his Doctrine: whereas when they perceive him careful to instruct them, and go before them, in whatever is their Duty to do, they will hearken to him

[d] 1 Pet. iii. 9.   [e] Heb. xiii. 17.   [f] Tit. ii. 2, 7.

with

with great Regard, when he cautions them against overdoing; and be unlikely to seek for imaginary Improvements abroad from Irregularities and Extravagances, whilst they experience themselves really improved at Home in an orderly established Method.

But then, to improve them effectually to their future Happiness, as well as to silence false Accusers, you must be assiduous in teaching the Principles, not only of Virtue and natural Religion, but of the Gospel: and of the Gospel, not as almost explained away by modern Refiners, but *as the Truth is in Jesus*[s]; as it is taught by the Church, of which you are Members; as you have engaged, by your Subscriptions and Declarations, that you will teach it yourselves. You must preach to them Faith in the ever-blessed Trinity: and vindicate, when it is requisite, those Parts of our Creeds and Offices which relate to that Article, from the very unjust Imputations of Absurdity and Uncharitableness which have been cast upon them. You must set forth the original Corruption of our Nature: our Redemption,

[s] Eph. iv. 21.

according

according to God's eternal Purpose in Christ [h], by the Sacrifice of the Cross; our Sanctification by the Influences of the Divine Spirit; the Insufficiency of our own good Works, and the Efficacy of Faith to Salvation: yet handling these Points in a doctrinal, not controversial Manner, unless particularly called to it; and even then treating Adversaries with Mildness and Pity, not with Bitterness or immoderate Vehemence.

The Truth, I fear, is, that many, if not most of us, have dwelt too little on these Doctrines in our Sermons: by no means, in general, from disbelieving or slighting them; but partly from knowing, that formerly they had been inculcated beyond their Proportion, and even to the Disparagement of Christian Obedience; partly from fancying them so generally received and remembered, that little needs to be said, but on social Obligations; partly again from not having studied Theology deeply enough, to treat of them ably and beneficially: God grant it may never have been for Want of inwardly experiencing their Im-

[h] Eph. iii. 11.

portance. But whatever be the cauſe, the Effect hath been lamentable. Our People have grown leſs and leſs mindful, firſt of the diſtinguiſhing Articles of their Creed, then, as will always be the Caſe, of that one, which they hold in common with the Heathens; have forgot in Effect their Creator as well as their Redeemer and Sanctifier; ſeldom or never ſeriouſly worſhipping him, or thinking of the State of their Souls in Relation to him; but flattering themſelves, that what they are pleaſed to call a moral and harmleſs Life, though far from being either, is the *one Thing needful.* Reflections have been made upon us, of different Natures, and with different Views, on Account of theſe Things, by Deiſts, by Papiſts, by Brethren of our own, which it is eaſy to ſhew have been much too ſevere. But the only complete Vindication of ourſelves will be to preach fully and frequently the Doctrines, which we are unjuſtly accuſed of caſting off or undervaluing: yet ſo, as to reſerve always a due Share of our Diſcourſes, which it is generally reported ſome of our Cenſurers do not, for the common Duties of common Life, as did our Saviour

and

and his Apoſtles. But then we muſt enforce them chiefly by Motives peculiarly Chriſtian: I will not ſay, only by ſuch; for the Scripture adds others. And while we urge on our Hearers the Neceſſity of univerſal Holineſs, we muſt urge equally that of their *being found in Chriſt; not having their own Righteouſneſs, which is of the Law, but the Righteouſneſs, which is of God by Faith*[l].

Copious and intereſting as the Subject is, I muſt now conclude. And *I beſeech you, Brethren, ſuffer the Word of Exhortation*[k]: for I have ſpoken to you from the Simplicity of a plain Heart, and the Sincerity of a deep Concern for the Intereſts of the Church of Chriſt, and the everlaſting Welfare of every one of you: not as condemning, not as diſeſteeming you, very far from it, but as being *jealous over you with godly Jealouſy*, and deeply affected with the preſent State of Religion amongſt us. Wickedneſs, Profaneneſs, avowed infidelity, have made a dreadful Progreſs in this Nation. The civil Power, in moſt Caſes, doth little to check that Progreſs: and it is an Unhappineſs in our moſt

[l] Phil. iii. 9.   [k] Heb. xiii. 22.

happy

happy Constitution, that it cannot easily, if at all, do what one might wish. Ecclesiastical Authority is not only too much limited but too much despised, as Matters now stand amongst us, to do almost any Thing to Purpose. In the small Degree, that it can be exerted usefully, I hope it will, and promise my utmost Endeavours, in all Cases notified to me, that it shall. But the main Support of Piety and Morals consists in the parochial Labours of the Clergy. If our Country is to be preserved from utter Profligateness and Ruin, it must be by our Means: and, take Notice, we cannot lose our Influence, but in a great Measure by our own Fault. If we look on what we are apt to call our Livings only as our Livelihoods, and think of little more than living on the Income of them according to our own Inclinations: if, for Want of *a good Conscience or Faith unfeigned*[1], we forfeit the Protection of God; and by Worldliness, or Indolence, or Levity in Behaviour, Talk, or Appearance, (for gross Vices I put out of the Question) lose, as we assured shall, the

[1] 1 Tim. i. 5.

Reverence

Reverence of Mankind: there will be no Foundation left for us to stand upon. Our legal Establishment will shake and sink under us, if once it can be said we do the Public little Service; and much sooner if we are suspected of disquieting it. Wicked People will attack us without Reserve; the good will be forced to condemn and give us up: and well would it be for us if this were the worst. *It is a small Thing to be judged of Man's Judgment: He, that judgeth us, is the Lord*[m]. But while we teach the genuine Truths of the Gospel, and evidently feel the Truths we teach; and are more anxious about the Souls of Men, than our own Profit, or Pleasure, or Power; while we submit ourselves dutifully and affectionately, (as we never had greater Cause) to the *King* and those *who are* put *in Authority* under him; *lead quiet and peaceable Lives in all Godliness and honesty*[n]; and join to our Piety and Loyalty and Virtue, but a common share of Prudence: we shall, in Spite of Enemies, through his Mercy, who hath promised to be *with us alway*[o], not fail of being upheld,

[m] 1 Cor. iv. 3, 4. [n] 1 Tim. ii. 2. [o] Matth. xxviii. 20.

The

The religious will *esteem us very highly in Love for our Work's Sake*[p]: the *wise in their Generation*[q], though not religious, will perceive our Importance: the vicious and destitute of Principle will be awed by us: and the Seed of the Word, however trampled under Foot by some, will spring up and bear Fruit in the Hearts of many. Let us think then seriously, what depends on us, what it requires of us, *and give ourselves wholly to it*[r]. God hath placed us in a Station of Difficulty and Labour, at present also of Reproach and Contempt from great Numbers of Men. But still, if we only learn to value our Function justly, and love it sincerely, we shall be unspeakably happier in discharging the Duties of it, than we possibly can be in any Thing else. The Things, in which the World places Happiness, are very Trifles. We may plainly see them to be such now, if we will: and we shall see in a little Time, whether we will or not, that the only real Point of Moment is, to have approved ourselves *good and faithful Ser-*

[p] 1 Thess. v. 13. [q] Luke xvi. 8.
[r] 1 Tim. iv. 15.

vants[s] to our great Master. Let us all therefore bear in Mind continually, how Matters will appear to us then; and heartily pray and earnestly endeavour, *so to pass through Things temporal, that we finally lose not the Things eternal.* Grant this, O heavenly Father, for Jesus Christ's Sake, our Lord[t].

---

[s] Matth. xxv. 21.   [t] Coll. 4th Sunday after Trinity.

A CHARGE

A CHARGE

DISTRIBUTED TO THE

CLERGY of the DIOCESE

OF

CANTERBURY,

In the YEAR 1762.

The ARCHBISHOP being hindered by Illness from visiting them in Person.

Reverend Brethren,

IT having pleased God that I should live to come amongst you a second Time, I think it my Duty to proceed with the same Kind of Exhortations, which I gave you at first. For though many Subjects of Instruction might be proper, there is a peculiar Propriety in those, which relate more immediately to your Conduct: and though I might very justly give you, in general, Praise instead of Advice, yet they who deserve the most of the former, will be most desirous of the latter, knowing how much Need of it the best of us have. And I hope the Freedoms which I shall take with you in this Respect, will the rather be pardoned, as I both permit and intreat you to use the same with me, when Occasion requires it; being sincerely disposed,

disposed, if I know myself, to set you an Example of Docility.

I began with your Obligation to Residence; and the Appointment of Curates, either to supply your Absence when you could not reside, or to assist you when the Work was too heavy for you. And then I entered a little into the common Duties of Incumbents and Curates, in which I shall now make some further Progress: more solicitous about the Importance of Directions, than the Accuracy of Method; and using no other Apology, if I should happen to repeat what I have given you in Charge already, than that of the Apostle: *To say the same Things, to me is not grievous, and for you it is safe*[a].

The same Apostle's Admonition to *Timothy* is, *Take Heed unto thyself, and to the Doctrine*[b]. The main Point is what he begins with, the Care of our Temper and Behaviour. For without that, our Preaching will seldom be such as it ought, and scarce ever bring forth its proper Fruits. Now a Christian Temper consists of various Parts: but the first Impression, which a genuine Faith in

[a] Phil. iii. 1.   [b] 1 Tim. iv. 16.

the Gospel makes on the Soul, and the ruling Principle, which it fixes there, is a deep Sense of Love to God and our Fellow-creatures, producing an earnest Desire, that we and they may be, for ever happy in his Presence. Whoever therefore is destitute of this Feeling, ought not, though free from gross Vices, to become a Clergyman: and without obtaining it from the Giver of all good Things by fervent Prayer, no Man is qualified to fill the Place of one. For notwithstanding that he may preserve some *Form of Godliness*, without which he would be mischievous and shocking in the highest Degree: yet not having the Reality and *Power thereof*[c], he must profess, and seemingly attempt to make others what he is far from being himself. Consequently his Endeavours out of the Pulpit will be infrequent, reluctant, faint: and in it they will at best be unnatural and ungraceful, whatever Pains he may take in his Compositions, or whatever Vehemence he may affect in his Delivery. Hence he will be dissatisfied within, detected and disesteemed by the judi-

[c] 2 Tim. iii. 5.

cious Part of his Hearers, and of little Use to the rest, if he is not even hurtful by misleading them. Or whatever his Case may be amongst Men, his inward Want of the Piety, which he outwardly pretends to, must render him uncommonly guilty in the Sight of God. Heaven forbid, that I should have Need to enlarge on such a Character in this Audience.

But have we not most of us Cause to apprehend, that our religious Principles, though sincere, are not sufficiently exerted; and therefore produce not the Fruit, which they might? Do we not rather take it for granted, that we approve ourselves to be duly in earnest, than find on impartial Examination, that we do? No Man should rashly say or surmise this of another: but every one should search Home into it for himself. And we should attentively read the Scriptures, and the Treatises written by wise and good Men concerning the Duties of God's Ministers: to see if we are such as they describe, and stir up ourselves to become such as we ought.

Good Inclinations, thus excited, will not fail,

fail, through the Affistance of divine Grace, of directing us into a suitable Conduct. And were a Man, who confessedly means well, to overdo a little sometimes, the Rightness of his Intention would plead his Excuse very strongly. However, we should carefully avoid Extremes, even on the better Side: not give uncommanded Demonstrations of our Christian Zeal, when they will probably serve no good Purpose, and be deemed Ostentation, or turned into Ridicule, or provoke ill Humour: but restrain, according as Times and Places and Company may require, the Sentiments which else we could be glad to utter. Only we must do this in such a Manner, as not to tempt the most rigid Professor of Religion to imagine, or the most profligate Enemy of it to suggest, that we have little or none: but shew our Concern for it on every fit Occasion, with full as much Diligence, as we decline unfit ones. And here, I conceive, it is, that we of the Clergy are chiefly apt to fail. We do not always appear in the common Intercourses of Life, sufficiently penetrated with the Importance of our Function, or

sufficiently

sufficiently assiduous to promote the Ends of our Mission.

Too possibly a great Part of our People may like the lukewarm amongst us the better for resembling themselves, and giving them no Uneasiness on Comparison, but seeming to authorize their Indifference. But then, such of us can do them no Good. Our Example can teach them Nothing beyond a little decent Regularity, in which they will fancy they need not quite come up to us neither. Our Sermons, and reading of Prayers, they will consider only as Matters of Form: and finding in us hardly any Thing at other Times of what we express at these, they will presume, that our inward Regard to it is not very great, and that they are not bound to have more. Therefore if they are pleased with us, if they esteem us, while we continue to be of this Turn, it must be for something foreign from our Office, something of a middle, or it may be a blameable Nature, not as Teachers of the Gospel: a Character which they take us to lay aside as much as we well can. And so the better they think of Us, the more lightly they

they will think of our Minister; till at length they join with those avowed Infidels, who boldly affirm, though often against their own Consciences, that we believe not what we preach, else it would have more Influence upon us.

Then, at the same Time, the right Dispositions of well inclined Persons will languish and decay, for Want of that Countenance and Assistance in serious Piety, which they should receive from their Pastors. For if the Tokens of our Piety be confined to the Church, they will be of little Service either out of it, or in it. Or if some good People suffer no Harm themselves from our Defects, they will see with great Sorrow that others do: all of them will be much readier to think the Clerical Order in general careless and light, if those are so, of whom they see most: their Ears will be open to the Invectives, which artful or heated Men are daily pouring forth against us; they will easily be led to undervalue and misconstrue the best Instructions of those, with whom they are disgusted; and run after any Teachers, who have the powerful Recommendation, for

it

it will always, and no Wonder, be a very powerful one, of feeming more in earneft. The Irregularities and Divifions which have prevailed fo lamentably in our Church of late, are greatly owing to an Opinion, that we are ufually indifferent about vital inward Religion. It is true, the Spreaders of this Imputation, which hath been monftroufly exaggerated, will have much to anfwer for: but fo fhall we alfo, unlefs we take the only Way to filence it, by cutting off hereafter all Occafion for it.

Now the firft neceffary Step to feem good is to be fo; for mere Pretence will be feen through: and the next is, to *let your Light fhine before Men*[d], in the faithful and laborious Exercife of your function. Living amongft your Parifhoners, or as near them as may be: inquiring frequently and perfonally concerning the Welfare and Behaviour of thofe, with whom you cannot be ftatedly prefent; reverent and judicious Reading of the Prayers and Leffons in your Churches, inftructive and affecting Sermons delivered with difcreet Warmth, Readinefs to take extraor-

[d] Matt. v. 16.

dinary Pains for the occasional Assistance of your Brethren, Diligence in forming the Youth to a Sense of their Christian Duty, in bringing your People to the holy Communion, and where it can be, to Week-Day Prayers: all these Thing will tend very much both to your Usefulness and your Credit. Relieving or obtaining Relief for such as are distressed in their Circumstances: hearing your People willingly and patiently, though perhaps low in Rank or weak in Understanding, when they would consult you upon any Difficulty, and answering them with Consideration and Tenderness: disposing them to be visited when sick, praying by them with Fervency, exhorting and comforting them with Fidelity, Compassion and Prudence; and reminding them strongly, yet mildly, after their Recovery, of their good Thoughts and Purposes during their Illness; will be further Proofs, very beneficial and very engaging ones, of your Seriousness: which however you must complete by going through every other Office of Religion with Dignity. I will specify two.

One

One is that of Baptism: which, especially when administered in private Houses without Necessity, is too often treated, even during the Administration, rather as an idle Ceremony than a Christian Sacrament: or however that be, is commonly close followed by very unsuitable, if not otherwise also indecent Levity and Jollity. Now in these Circumstances it is highly requisite, that the Minister should, by a due Mixture of Gravity and Judgement, support the Solemnity of the Ordinance; and either prevent Improprieties in the Sequel, or if it be doubtful whether he can, excuse himself, with a civil Intimation of the Unfitness of them, from being present. The other Instance is, that of saying Grace over our daily Food: which many, if not most, of the Laity have, with a Profaneness more than heathenish, laid aside: and I am sorry to add, that some of the Clergy hurry it over so irreverently, in a Mutter or a Whisper, scarce, if at all, intelligible, that one might question, whether they had not better lay it aside too, which yet God forbid, than make it thus insignificant; and expose to Contempt an Act of Devotion, and themselves along with it, as doing what they are ashamed of.

Indeed far from authorizing any Slights of this Sort by our Example, and as it were our Consent, we must through our whole Conversation steadily and resolutely, though with Mildness and Modesty, always keep up the Honour of Religion and our Order, which is inseparable from our own: never speak a Word, or use a Gesture, which can with the least Colour be interpreted, as if we had small Regard to our Profession, or exercised it chiefly for a Maintenance: never repeat, never hear, Discourses of an irreligious or immoral Turn, without expressing a plain Disapprobation, briefly or at large, as the Case may require: yet be on all Occasions courteous, and on proper Occasions cheerful; but let it be evidently the Cheerfulness of serious Men. *Foolish Talking and Jesting are not convenient*[e], not becoming any Person: but those least of all, who should know best, that *every idle Word which Men shall speak, they shall give an Account*

[e] Eph. v. 4.

thereof,

thereof, according to its Tendency, *in the Day of Judgment* [f]. Unseasonable or excessive Mirth sits peculiarly ill upon him whose Office must or ought to bring before his Mind so frequently, the Afflictions of this mortal State, the Holiness of God's Law, his own grievous Imperfections, the deplorable Sins of many others, and the final Sentence, that awaits us all. Doubtless we should endeavour to make Religion agreeable; but not to make ourselves agreeable, by leading our Company to forget Religion. We should *every one of us please his Neighbour for his Good* [g]: but not so *please Men*, as to fail in the Character of *Servants of Christ* [h]. We should be *made*, in a fitting Sense and Measure, *all Things to all Men, that we may by all Means save some* [i]: but we shall lose ourselves, not save others, if we are quite different Persons in the Pulpit and out of it: nor can we act a more incongruous Part, than to chuse raising and promoting the Laugh for our Province in Conversation, instead of duly restraining our own Liveli-

[f] Matt. xii. 36.   [g] Rom. xv. 2.   [h] Gal. i. 10.
[i] 1 Cor. ix. 22.

ness and that of others. *For out of the Abundance of the Heart the Mouth speaketh* [k] : and our Hearts ought to abound with better Things. I own, both affected and excessive Restraint will do Harm. But if we are sincerely pious, and endeavour to be prudent, we shall combine useful Informations and Reflections with harmless Entertainment: our *Speech will be with Grace, seasoned with Salt, that we may know how we ought to answer every Man* [l] : we shall prove that we have the End of our Ministry constantly in View, by drawing profitable Lessons, frequently, but naturally, out of Topics of Indifference; and bringing back the Discourse, if it goes astray, from exceptionable or unsafe Subjects, to innocent ones; yet if possible without offensive Reproof, and perhaps imperceptibly. *For the Servant of the Lord must not strive*, that is, roughly, and harshly, *but be gentle unto all Men* [m], even the worst. Yet on the other Hand servile Obsequiousness, or *flattering Words* [n], even to the best, are far remote from *having*

[k] Matth. xii. 34.   [l] Col. iv. 6.   [m] 2 Tim. ii. 24.
[n] 1 Thess. ii. 5.

our *Conversation in Simplicity and godly Sincerity*°.

Talking with great Earnestness about worldly Affairs, or with great Delight about Diversions and Trifles, betrays a Mind over-much set upon them: and Numbers will represent the Case, as worse than it is. Nay, our being only in a very peculiar Degree good Judges of such Matters, or of any that are unconnected with our Office, will, unless we have some especial Call to them, be commonly thought to imply, that we have studied and love them beyond what we ought, to the Neglect of our proper Business. For we are not to expect very favourable Constructions from Mankind: yet it greatly imports us to have their good Opinion; which we shall not secure, unless in whatever other Lights they may see us occasionally, the worthy Clergyman be the predominant Part of our Character. If practical Christian Piety and Benevolence and Self Government, with constant Zeal to promote them all upon Earth, are not the first and chief Qualities, which your

° 2 Cor. i. 12.

Parishioners

Parishioners and Acquaintance will ascribe to you; if they will speak of you, as noted on other Accounts, but pass over these Articles; and when asked about them, be at a Loss what to say; excepting possibly that they know no Harm of you; all is not right: nor can such a Clergy answer the Design of its Institution any where; or even maintain its Ground in a Country of Freedom and Learning, though a yet worse may in the Midst of Slavery and Ignorance.

Actually sharing in the Gaieties and Amusements of the World will provoke Censure still more, than making them favourite Subjects of Discourse. I do not say, that Recreations, lawful in themselves, are unlawful to us: or that those which have been formerly prohibited by ecclesiastical Rules, merely as disreputable, may not cease to be so by Change of Custom. But still *not all Things lawful are expedient* [f], and certainly these Things, further than they are in Truth requisite for Health of Body, Refreshment of Mind, or some really valuable Purpose, are all a Misemployment of our leisure

[f] 1 Cor. vi. 12.

Hours, which we ought to set our People a Pattern of filling up well. A Minister of God's Word, attentive to his Duty, will neither have Leisure for such Dissipations, public or domestic, nor Liking to them. He will see, that Pleasure, or rather a wretched Affectation of it, is become the Idol of Mankind; to which they are sacrificing their Fortunes, their Families, their Healths, their Reputations, their Regard to God, to their social Duties, to the State of their Souls, to their future Being. Now what are the Clergy to do in this Case? If we but seem to go along with them, who shall call them back? For as to the Pretence of keeping them within Bounds by our Presence; it is visibly a mere Pretence. Or were it not, the older and graver of us would surely think such a Superintendency no very honourable one: and few of the younger and livelier could be safely trusted with it. Indeed we none of us know, into what Improprieties of Behaviour, at least what Wrongness of Disposition we may be drawn by the *evil Communications* of these Assemblies: whether, if happily they should not otherwise

corrupt

corrupt our *good Manners* [q], we may not however grow inwardly fond of them; come to think our profession a dull one, and the Calls of it troublesome; throw off as much of the Burthen as we can, and perform with Reluctance and cold Formality the Remainder, which we must.

At least it will be suspected, that we cannot greatly disapprove the Customs in which we voluntarily join, the Persons with whom we familiarly associate, or indeed any Thing said or done where we delight to be: that if we do not go the utmost Lengths, yet we should, if for Shame we durst: for these Things are our Choice, not the Duties of our Ministry; which therefore Declaimers will say we are not sincere in, or however unfit for. And even they, who plead our Example as a Precedent for themselves, will usually honour us much the less for setting it.

Still I do not mean, that we should be sour and morose; condemn innocent Relaxations, and provoke men to say, that we rail out of Envy at what we have absurdly tied

[q] 1 Cor. xv. 33.

up ourselves from partaking of: but express our Dislike of them as mildly as the Case will bear; slight with good Humour the Indulgences, in which others falsely place their Happiness; and convince them by our Experience as well as Reasoning, how very comfortably they may live without them. It is true, paying Court to the gay and inconsiderate by Imitation of them, may often be the shorter, and sometimes the surer Way to their Favour. But the Favour of the fashionable World is not our Aim: if it be, we have chosen our Profession very unwisely. And though we should succeed thus with such Persons in Point of Interest, we must not hope even for their Esteem. For they will both think and speak with the lowest Contempt of the complying Wretch, whom yet for their own Convenience or Humour they will caress, and now and then prefer.

Our Predecessors, that their abstaining from indiscreet Levities might be notorious, wore constantly the peculiar Habit of their Order. And certainly we should be more respected, if we followed their Example in this

this more univerfally. They complained of no Inconveniencies from it: nor did I ever, in a Courfe of many Years, find any worth naming. In the primitive and perfecuting Times indeed Clergymen wore no peculiar Drefs: and long after were diftinguifhed only by retaining a greater Simplicity of Garb than others. But gradually Superiors difcerned Reafons for enjoying a different Sort: and furely others may well pay them fo far the Obedience promifed to them, as always to fhew by fome evident and proper Marks, (for Nothing more is expected) of what Clafs of Men they are. If you do not, it will be faid, either that you are afhamed of your Caufe, or confcious of your Unfkilfulnefs to defend it, or that you conceal yourfelves to take occafionally unfit Liberties. Indeed fome external Reftraints of this Kind, merely as an Admonition againft unfeemly Difcourfe and Conduct and Company, would, though not prefcribed, be very advifeable for young Clergymen: amongft whom they, who diflike them the moft, might fometimes perceive, that they have the moft need of them. And we
that

that are older, should keep up the Custom for their Sakes, though unnecessary for our own. Besides, we may all prevent, by such Notification of ourselves, a great deal of unbecoming Talk and Deportment in others: and so escape both the Disagreeableness of reproving it, and the Impropriety of not reproving it. Or, if after all it cannot be prevented, they who are offended with it, will immediately see in us a Refuse from it.

But then a Habit, visibly a Clergyman's, must be such in every Part as befits a Clergyman: have no Look of Effeminacy or Love of Finery in it[r]. For we had better put on the Lay Dress intirely, than disgrace the Clerical one. And it is doubly contemptible, first to shew what a Fondness we have for Things utterly beneath us, and then how poorly we are able to indulge it. Therefore let us be uniform: and as our Character is a truly venerable one, let us think we do ourselves Honour by wearing the ancient Badges of it. I need not add, that our whole Demeanour should be answerable to

---

[r] *Hieron. ad Nepotian.* §. 9.

our Cloathing: that Softness and Delicacy of Manner, Skill in the Science of Eating*, and the Perfection of Liquors, in short every Approach to luxurious Gratification, is strangely out of Place in one, who hath devoted himself to *endure Hardness as a good Soldier of Jesus Christ*ᵗ.

Still we ought to judge very charitably of those, who take greater Liberties, than we dare: never blame them more, seldom so much as they deserve; and confine our Severity to our own Practice. Only we must watch with moderate Strictness over our Families also: not only keeping up the joint separate Worship of God in them, which I hope no Clergyman omits, but forming them to every part of Piety and Virtue and Prudence. St. *Paul* requires, that not only *Deacons*, but their *Wives* be *grave*ᵘ: and that the higher Clergy be such, as *rule well their own Houses, having their Children in Subjection with all Gravity: for if a Man know not how to rule his own House, how shall he take Care of the Church*

---

* Hieron. ad Nepotian. §. 6.   ᵗ 2 Tim, ii. 3.   ᵘ 1 Tim. iii. 8, 11.

of God[w]*?* Whence we have all promised at our Ordination, to *frame and fashion our Families,* together with ourselves, *according to the Doctrine of Christ, and to make them, as much as in us lieth, wholesome Examples and Patterns to his Flock.* They are naturally the first Objects of our Care: we have peculiar Opportunities of instructing and restraining them. If we neglect them, we shall never be thought to have much Concern for others: if we are unsuccessful with them, we shall be deemed very unskilful; and bid to look at Home before we reprove the rest of our Flock. But exhibiting Instances of Goodness and Happiness, produced under our own Roofs by the Methods, to which we direct those around us, must needs add singular Weight to our Exhortations.

For the Importance of the Rules hitherto laid down, we have the Judgment of a most able and subtle and determined enemy, the Emperor *Julian:* who designing to re-establish Paganism, and accounting, as he declares, the Strictness and Sanctity, professed by Christians, to be a principal Cause of the Prevalence

---

[w] 1 Tim. v. 4, 5.

of their Faith, in two of his Epistles gives Directions, undoubtedly copied from the Injunctions observed by the Clergy of those Days, that the Heathen Priests be Men of serious Tempers and Deportment; that they neither utter, nor hear, nor read, nor think of any Thing licentious or indecent; that they banish far from them all offensive Jests and libertine Conversation: be neither expensive nor shewish in their Apparel; go to no Entertainments but such as are made by the worthiest Persons; frequent no Taverns: appear but seldom in Places of Concourse; never be seen at the public Games and Spectacles; and take Care that their Wives and Children and Servants be pious, as well as themselves[x]. Let not, I entreat you, this Apostate put us to Shame.

But Clergymen, who are serious in their whole Behaviour, and the Care of their Families also, are often too unactive amongst their People: apt to think, that if they perform regularly the ordinary Offices of the Church, exhort from the Pulpit such

[x] Ep. 49. ad *Arsac*. P. 430, 431. Fragm. Ep. p. 301—305.

as will come to hear them, and anſwer the common occaſional Calls of parochial Duty they have done as much as they need or well can, and ſo turn themſelves to other Matters: perhaps never viſit ſome of their Pariſhioners; and with the reſt enter only into the ſame Sort of Talk, that any one elſe would do. Now St. *Paul* ſaith he *taught* the Epheſians both *publicly and from Houſe to Houſe, teſtifying Repentance toward God, and Faith toward our Lord Jeſus Chriſt*ʸ; and *ceaſed not to warn every one Day and Night*ᶻ. He alſo commands *Timothy* to *preach the Word*, and *be inſtant in Seaſon and out of Seaſon*ᵃ; at ſtated Times and others; not forcing Advice upon Perſons, when it was likelier to do Harm than good: but prudently improving leſs favourable Opportunities, if no others offered. Thus unqueſtionably ſhould we do. And a chief Reaſon, why we have ſo little Hold upon our People is, that we converſe with them ſo little, as Watchmen over their Souls. The Paſtors of the foreign Proteſtants out do us gteatly in this Reſpect, and are honoured in

ʸ Acts xx. 20, 21. ᶻ Ver. 31. ᵃ 2 Tim. iv. 2.

Proportion.

Proportion. The Romish Priests have their Laity under their Hands, on one Account or another, almost continually, and acquire by it an absolute Dominion over them. Both the old Dissenters from our Church, and those who are now forming new Separations, gain and preserve a surprising Influence amongst their Followers by personal religious Intercourse. Why should not we learn from them? At first such Applications may by Disuse appear strange; and have both their Difficulties and their Dangers. But the most apprehensive of them will be the safest from them; and all will improve their Talents by Practice. On young Persons you will be able to make good Impressions by Discourse with them before Confirmation; these may be renewed in private exhortations afterwards to receive the Sacrament: and the spiritual Acquaintance, thus begun, may be continued ever after. Other Means may be found with grown Persons: on the first settling of a Family in your Parish; on Occasion of any great Sickness, or Affliction, or Mercy; on many others, if you seek for them, and engage worthy Friends to assist you. Even
common

common Conversation may be led very natural to Points of Piety and Morals; and Numbers be induced thus to reading proper Books, to public, to private, to Family Devotion, to Sobriety, Justice, Alms-giving and Christian Love. When once you are well got into the Method, you will proceed with Ease and Applause; provided your whole Character and Conduct be consistent, else you will fall into total Disgrace; and particularly provided you convince your Parishioners, that you *seek, not theirs, but them* [b].

A due Measure of Disinterestedness is one main Requisite for the success of a Clergyman's Labours. You will therefore avoid all mean Attention to small Matters: never be rigorous in your Demands of them; never engage in any Disputes about them, unless a Part of your Income, too large to be given up, depends upon them. In all Disputes you will prefer discreet References to Proceedings at Law: and when the latter become necessary, carry them on in the fairest, the least expensive, the friendliest Manner.

[b] 2 Cor. xii. 14.

You will be very tender in your Demands upon the poor, and very equitable towards the rich; though you will confcientioufly preferve all the material Rights, with which you are intrufted, for your Succeffors. If you find Room and Reafon to improve your Income, you will do it within Bounds: and prove, that no wrong Motive induces you to it, by living with decent Frugality, providing for your Families with Moderation, and going as far as ever you are able in Acts of good-natured, and efpecially of pious, Liberality; which are the moft valuable in themfelves, the moft incumbent on you, and the moft overlooked by others. For Nothing gives greater or jufter Offence, than to fee a Clergyman intent upon hoarding, or luxurious, or fplendid, inftead of being charitable.

Few indeed of our Order have much to fpare : and many have Caufe to wifh for a more plentiful Subfiftence. Yet even thefe, and much more the better preferred, if they are earneft feekers and importunate Solicitors for Promotion, lower their Characters grievoufly: and fuch as ufe indirect Means to obtain it, are often providentially difappointed;

pointed; or though they succeed, always dishonour themselves, and never do much Good to others: whereas the lowest of their Brethren will be justly respected, and may be highly useful, if he submits contentedly to God's good Providence, and labours to live within the Compass of his Income: exceeding which, without visible Necessity, will bring some Imputations even upon him, and deservedly a much heavier on such as enjoy an ampler Provision.

However inoffensive we are, we must expect to receive, from Time to Time, injurious and provoking Treatment, as the Scripture hath forewarned us. We shall hurt both our own Cause and that of Religion dreadfully, if we return it: and do Honour to both, if we behave under it calmly, *with such Meekness of Wisdom* [c], as may tend to bring our Adversaries over, if not to our Sentiments concerning the Matter in Question, whatever it be, yet to a good Opinion of our Meaning and Temper; or may at least, if we fail of Success with them, engage more impartial Persons to countenance and protect us.

[c] James iii. 13.

us. Indeed we ought, if possible, to keep not only ourselves, but others, out of all angry Contests. We solemnly promised at our Ordination, to *maintain and set forwards, as much as lieth in us, Quietness, Peace and Love among all Christian People, and especially among them that are or shall be committed to our Charge:* and by so doing, we are bound never to raise or foment personal, family, parochial, political, or ecclesiastical Animosities, but do all in our Power to compose and extinguish them: nor will any Thing conduce more to our Credit or to our Usefulness. The political Party-Spirit is, God be thanked, of late Years much abated. Let us guard against the Return of it: shew, in Word and Deed, becoming Respect, as we have great Cause, to our excellent King, and all who are put in Authority under him: *not exercise ourselves in Matters too high for us*[d], but *be quiet and do our own Business*[e]; *let our Moderation, even where we are concerned to meddle, be known unto all Men*[f]; exercising it even to

[d] Psal. cxxxi. 2. [e] 1 Thess. iv. 11. [f] Phil. iv. 4.

those who have least of it; and always remember, that neither Patriot Love to our earthly Country, nor loyal Attachment to our earthly Sovereign, will be accepted by our heavenly Father, without uniform Obedience to the Whole of his Gospel.

Another Point of great Importance to Clergymen is, that they be studious. This will keep your Money from being spent unwisely; and likewise your Time from being thrown away hurtfully or unprofitably, or hanging heavy on your Hands. It will procure you Reverence too, as Persons of Knowledge: whereas the idle will, even by the ignorant, be thought deficient. And which is the main Thing, this alone will enable you to understand the Business of your Station, and perform it well. But then you must apply to such Things chiefly, as will fit you most to answer the great End of your Employment; and *determine* with St. Paul *to know Nothing,* comparatively speaking *amongst* your People, *save Christ Jesus and him crucified*[g]. The Concern of a Parish Minister is, to make the lowest of his

[g] 1 Cor. ii. 2.

Congregation apprehend the Doctrine of Salvation by Repentance, Faith and Obedience; and to labour, that when they know the Way of Life, they may walk in it. If he doth not these Things for them, he doth Nothing: and it requires much Consideration to find out the proper Methods of doing them, and much Pains and Patience to try one after another. Smooth Discourses, composed partly in fine Words which they do not understand, partly in flowing Sentences which they cannot follow to the End; containing little that awakens their drowsy Attention, little that inforces on them plainly and home what they must do to be saved; leave them as ignorant and unreformed as ever, and only lull them into a fatal Security. Therefore bring yourselves down to their Level; for what suits the meanest Christian will suit the highest: examine if they take in what you say, and change the Form of it till they do. This I recommend for your first Study: and be assured, you will improve yourselves by it no less than your Hearers. But so far as you have Opportunity consistently with this,

apply

apply to any Part of Science, to every Part you can, that is connected with your Profeſſion: only learn, by weighing carefully the Judgments and Reaſonings of others, to think modeſtly of yourſelves: avoid, in the Outſet of your Inquiries more eſpecially, drawing haſty Concluſions: be at leaſt as much on your Guard againſt Fondneſs of new Opinions, as Prepoſſeſſion for eſtabliſhed Doctrines: and beware of being miſled, either by the Poſitiveneſs of vehement Writers, or the falſe Colours of artful ones.

You will doubtleſs cultivate peculiarly thoſe Branches of Knowledge, which the Circumſtances of the Times, or of your Pariſhes, peculiarly point out to you. God hath permitted to us, for our Sins, to be attacked, in a remarkable Degree, by Infidels on one Hand, and by Maintainers of innumerable ſtrange Notions on the other. And we have Need, that every one, who is able to qualify himſelf well, ſhould aſſiſt in defending his Part of the common Cauſe. For there are too many unanſwered Books abroad in the World, and more appearing daily, written

written againſt Chriſtianity and Morals and the Doctrines of our Church. Nor have we of the Clergy, for ſome Time paſt, borne ſo large a Share, comparatively with Perſons of other Communions, in vindicating what we teach, as might be expected from us. I hope you are not often obliged, in this Dioceſe, to encounter Unbelievers from the Pulpit: and you will certainly not chuſe to alarm your People, by refuting, in Form, Objections to which they are Strangers; though it may be uſeful to obviate them briefly, and if poſſible without naming them. But as, probably enough, ſome of you will at one Time or another in Company meet with ſuch Perſons, or hear of their Talk, I would give you a few Directions in Relation to them.

If any of them are virtuous in their Conduct, and backward to offend in Diſcourſe, they ſhould not be unſeaſonably provoked, but treated with Reſpect. If any of them build their Unbelief on ſerious Argument, which plainly very few do, they ſhould be directed to the Books, or the learned Men, that are beſt fitted to anſwer them: and the less able should prepare for Combat with them, but not engage too far in it prematurely. If they cannot at present be convinced of the Falsehood of their Tenets, they should be shewn however, in a gentle Manner, the pernicious Effects of promulging them. But if they will obstinately persist to sacrifice every Thing valuable amongst Men to their own Vices, or their own Vanity, we must openly withstand them, and warn others against them. Yet even this ought to be done without Passion or Bitterness, otherwise all the Blame will be laid on us: especially without personal Incivilities, even to the worst of them, else they will become still worse than they were. But then we must never assist the very best of them in gaining Influence and growing dangerous; nor bring our own Sincerity into Question by Intimacies with them, which they will usually represent, and sometimes believe, to proceed from our inwardly thinking as they do. Much less should we ever condescend to the shocking Meanness of paying Court for private Ends, either to them, or to wicked Wretches of any Kind, though not Infidels; but

but connect ourselves with worthy Persons; engage their Support, and excite their Endeavours to repress Profaneness and Immorality.

It is peculiarly unhappy, that while we are employed on one Side in defending the Gospel, we are accused on another of corrupting it. I have not now in my View either the Church of *Rome*, or the Protestants who broke off from us a Century ago. The Methods of dealing with both have been long since prescribed, and I repeat them not: but intreat your Attention to the Movements of each, especially the former, if you have any of them in your Parishes. But I mean to speak of Persons risen up in our own Times, and professing the strictest Piety: who vehemently charge us with departing from the Doctrines and slighting the Precepts of our Religion: but have indeed themselves advanced unjustifiable Notions, as necessary Truths; giving good People groundless Fears, and bad ones groundless Hopes; disturbed the Understandings of some, impaired the Circumstances of others; prejudiced Multitudes against their proper Ministers, and prevented

prevented their Edification by them; produced firſt Diſorders in our Churches, then partial or total Sepaartions from them; and ſet up unauthorized Teachers in their Aſſemblies. Where theſe Irregularities will end, God only knows: but it behoves us to be very careful, that they make no Progreſs through our Fault.

Now it would not only be injurious, but profane, to brand, with an opprobrious Name, Chriſtians remarkably ſerious, merely for being ſuch: and equally imprudent to diſclaim them as not belonging to us, to let a Sect gain the Credit of them, and labour to drive them into it. Surely we ſhould take, even were they wavering, or actually gone from us, the moſt reſpectful and perſuaſive Means of recalling ſuch, and fixing them with us. Nay, ſuppoſing any Perſons irrecoverably gone, we ſhould not be haſty to condemn, even in our Thoughts, either them or their Party, as Enthuſiaſts or Hypocrites: *whatſoever they are, it maketh no Matter to us* [h]. And much leſs ought we to ſay of either worſe than we are ſure they

[h] Gal. ii. 6.

deſerve.

deserve. When we are undoubtedly well informed of any extravagant Things, which they have asserted or done, it may be useful to speak strongly of them: but not with Anger and Exaggeration; which will only give them a Handle to censure our Uncharitableness, and confute us: but with deep Concern, that when so few Persons express any Zeal for the Gospel, so many of those, who do, run into Extremes, that hurt its Interests. Nor will Ridicule become our Character, or serve our Cause better than Invective. It may please those very highly, who are in no Danger of being proselyted by them. But what shall we get by that? Persons negligent of Religion will at the same Time be confirmed in their Negligence; and think, that all they need to avoid is being *righteous overmuch*[i]. Tender Minds will be grieved and wounded by such ill-placed Levity: and crafty Declaimers will rail at us with Success, as *Scoffers*[k], *denying the Power of Godliness*[l]. But if we let fall any light Expressions, that can be wrested into a seeming Disrespect of any Scripture

[i] Eccl. vii. 16.   [k] 2 Pet. iii. 3.   [l] 2 Tim. ii. 15.

Doctrine

Doctrine or Phrase, we shall give our Adversaries unspeakable Advantages: and they have shewn, that they will use them without Mercy or Equity. Therefore we must guard every Word, that we utter, against Misrepresentations: be sure to express, in public and private, our firm Belief of whatever evangelical Truths border upon their Mistakes: and certainly be as vigilant over our Behaviour, as our Teaching: encourage no Violence, no Rudeness towards them; but recommend ourselves to them by our Mildness, our Seriousness, our Diligence: honour those, who are truly devout and virtuous amongst them, much more on that Account, than we blame them for being injudicious, and hard to please; and be full as ready to acknowledge the Good they have done, as to complain of the Harm: yet beware, and counsel others to beware, of being drawn, by Esteem of their Piety, into relishing their Singularities, and patronizing their Schism.

Acting thus, we shall not only *cut off Occasion from those who desire Occasion*[m] to

[m] 2 Cor. xi. 12.

speak

speak Evil of us, and be able to remonstrate with Authority and Effect against their Excesses and Wildnesses; but, which is the chief Point, we shall become better Ministers of Christ for their harsh Treatment of us. And we should always labour, that every Thing may have this Influence upon us: think with ourselves, if others go too far, whether we do not fall short; ask our Consciences, whether we really do all that is in our Power to reform and improve our People; whether the small Success of our Endeavours be, in Truth, as it ought, a heavy Grief to us; whether we have carefully searched out, and try incessantly to overcome the Difficulties that lie in our Way to making them better. These Things, if we are in earnest, we shall chiefly have at Heart: and if we are not in earnest, *we are of all Men* the most guilty, and *the most miserable* [n].

In giving you my Advice thus largely and freely on these several Heads, I no more suppose you culpable in Relation to any of them, than you do your Parishioners, when

[n] 1 Cor. xv. 19.

you exhort them to any particular Duties, or warn them against particular Sins. On the contrary, to use the Apostle's Words, *I am persuaded of you, Brethren, that ye are full of Goodness, replenished with all Knowledge, able also to admonish one another.* Nevertheless, if I may presume to adopt, with due Abatements, the subsequent Words also, *I have spoken somewhat boldly unto you in Part, as putting you in Mind, because of the Grace which is given you of God, that I should be the Minister of Jesus Christ to you*°, as you are to your respective Congregations. And let us all pray for ourselves and each other daily, that we may so *feed the Flock of God which is among us, and be Ensamples to it, that when the chief Shepherd shall appear, we may receive a Crown of Glory, that fadeth not away*[p].

° Rom. xv. 14, 15, 16.   [p] 1 Pet. v. 2, 3, 4.

A CHARGE

A CHARGE

DELIVERED TO THE

CLERGY of the DIOCESE

OF

CANTERBURY,

In the YEAR 1766.

Reverend Brethren,

HAVING diftributed amongft you, above three Years ago, when Sicknefs prevented me from vifiting you in Perfon, a printed Difcourfe, in which I exhorted you, as St. *Paul* did *Timothy*, to *take Heed unto yourfelves*; I proceed now to add, as he did, *and to your Doctrine*[a].

To inftruct Perfons in Religion is the leading Part of a Clergyman's Duty. And though he will do it in a very ufeful Degree by the Example of a Chriftian Behaviour on all Occafions; yet he will do it more efpecially in the particular Difcharge of his Office. When he is only to ufe the Forms prefcribed him, he may, by ufing them with due Reverence and Propriety, greatly promote both Knowledge and pious Difpofitions in his Hearers.

[a] 1 Tim. iv. 16.

Hearers. Therefore we ought to watch diligently over ourselves in this Respect: and then it will be easier to convince our People, that they may and should learn a great deal from the Exhortations, the Prayers, the Praises, the Portions of Scripture, of which our Liturgy consists; that therefore, even when there is no other Service, they should come to Church for the Sake of these far more constantly, and attend to them far more carefully, than the Generality of them do; indeed should have them in much higher Esteem, than the mere Products of our private Thoughts.

But I shall confine myself to the Instructions, which you give of your own; speaking of them chiefly with a View of suggesting such Advice to the younger Part of you, as I hope the elder will approve, and enforce.

And here I must begin with repeating, what I need not enlarge upon, for I have done it already, that the Foundation of every Thing in our Profession is true Piety within our Breasts, prompting us to excite it in others. Even Heathens made it a Rule, that

that an Orator, if he would perfuade, muſt be a good Man: much more muſt a Preacher. When a bad one utters divine Truths, we ſhut our Ears, we feel Indignation. From yourſelves therefore througnly, by devout Meditations and fervent Prayer, to Seriouſneſs of Heart, and Zeal for the eternal Welfare of Souls: for then every Thing elſe, that you are to do, will follow of Courſe.

You will earneſtly labour to complete yourſelves in all proper Knowledge: not merely the introductory Kinds, which unhappily are often almoſt the only ones, taught the Candidates for holy Orders; but thoſe chiefly, which have a cloſer Connection with your Work. And though, amongſt theſe, the Science of Morals and natural Religion is highly to be valued, yet the Doctrines and Precepts of the Goſpel require your principal Regard beyond all Comparison. It is of the Goſpel, that you are Miniſters: all other Learning will leave you eſſentially unqualified; and this alone comprehends every Thing, that is neceſſary. Without it, you will never *approve yourſelves to God, as Workmen that need not to be ashamed*[b], nor *make your Hearers wise unto Salvation*[c]. Therefore you must diligently peruse the holy Scriptures, and as much as you can of them in the Original; *that, as* the Office of Ordination expresses it, *by daily reading and weighing of them ye may wax riper and stronger in your Ministry.* And you must not grudge the Expence, which may surely be well spared in some other Things, of procuring, according to your Abilities, the Assistance, both of such Commentators, as will best shew you the true Sense of holy Writ; and of such also, as will best direct you, how to draw from it needful Instructions. General Systems of Theology, and particular Treatises on Points of Moment, will enlarge your Stock of Matter: and the most noted Sermons will be Patterns to you of Composition.

For I suppose the Discourses, even of those who have the lowest Qualifications, to be, in a great Measure at least, of their own Composition. Else they will seldom either sufficiently suit the Congregation to which

[b] 2 Tim. ii. 15.   [c] 2 Tim. iii. 15.

they are delivered, or be delivered in the Manner which they ought. Besides, if Persons decline taking this Trouble, they will probably also decline that of fitting themselves in other Ways for parochial Usefulness, and throw away their Time unwisely, if not worse. That will soon be observed to their Disadvantage; and if once it be suspected, that through Incapacity or Idleness they steal what they preach, they will have small Influence, if any. I do not mean, that no Use ought to be made of the Labours of others: for indeed I have made no little Use of them in what I am saying, and about to say. I would have young Clergymen, especially, make very great Use of the Works of able Divines: not inconsiderately and servilely transcribe them; but study, digest, contract, amplify, vary, adapt to their Purpose, improve, if possible, what they find in them. For thus it will fairly become their own; mix naturally with what proceeds altogether from themselves; and preserve their youthful Productions from the Imputation of being empty and jejune. In the Choice of such Authors you will consult religious and judicious Friends, always joining your own Experience. Those Writers, whom you find the most effectual to enlighten your Understandings, convince you of your Faults, animate you to good Resolutions, and guide and support you in the Execution of them, will best help you to produce the same Effect on others. These therefore imitate: but with Judgement. If, amidst their Excellencies, you observe Mistakes, Defects, Redundancies, Flights indiscreetly high, despicably familiar Condescensions, Sallies over-vehement; beware of adopting any of them. And remember too that a very close Imitation, of Singularities above all, will both betray you, and be disgustful.

When you go about to prepare an Instruction for your People, first consider carefully of a proper Subject and Text: begging God to direct your Choice, and dispose you to treat them in a proper Way. Chusing a Text, without Need, that will surprise, or seemingly a barren one, to shew what your Art can extract from it, will appear ingenious perhaps to some, but Vanity to most with good Reason. Chusing one, that requires much accommodating to your Purpose, is but mispending Pains and Time: and so is labouring to clear up a very obscure one, unless it be of great Importance. And giving a new Translation or Sense of a Text, unless the present hath considerable Inconveniencies, will only puzzle your Audience, and tempt them to doubt, whether they understand the rest of their Bible. Such a Text is most convenient, as will branch out of itself into the main Parts of your Discourse: but at least you should make it appear to be the Groundwork of your Discourse, and not an Afterthought.

Plan your Method in the Beginning of your Composition: but change it afterwards, if you see Cause. Never run the Matter of one Head into another, nor digress to any Thing foreign: for every Subject well considered, will afford you enough. It is usually best to propose your general Heads together, before you proceed upon them separately, and to give Notice when you come to each. Subdivisions also assist the Memory of the Hearer, if they are not too many: and passing from a former Head to the next by an easy Transition, is graceful. But a Disposition may be very orderly, without mentioning in Form the several Members, of which it consists: and sometimes that Formality prevents a Discourse from flowing with Freedom and Spirit. After the explanatory Part, Proofs from Reason and Scripture take the next Place; then Inferences, if any useful ones follow peculiarly from what hath preceded: and lastly Exhortations to suitable Practice, which can hardly ever be omitted, and ought to be such as may leave a durable Impression. The Length of Sermons, though it should always be moderate, may be very different at different Times. Only give no Room to think, that in a short one have you said but little; or in a long one have either said any Thing which was not pertinent, or dwelt upon any Thing beyond what was needful.

An indispensable Point throughout is to preserve Attention: for if that be not paid, all your Labour is lost. And Persons are singularly apt to be inattentive to Preachers. Our Subjects are, and ought to be, the most common

common and trite of any. And hence, unlefs we ufe a little honeft Art to prevent it, our People will think, will many of them find indeed, that they know beforehand moft of what we fhall deliver to them, and fo will foon grow weary of minding us. Coming to Church, the Bulk of Mankind, even ftill, confider as a Duty: but hearing as they ought, they partly negleƈt, and partly experience to be difficult. Therefore we muft not only admonifh, but affift them. For this End we muft fhew them from firft to laft, that we are not merely faying good Things in their Prefence, but direƈting what we fay to them perfonally, as a Matter which concerns them beyond Expreffion. More general Difcourfes they often want Skill to take Home to themfelves; and oftener yet Inclination: fo they fit all the while ftupidly regardlefs of what is delivered. Therefore we muft intereft them in it, by calling upon them to obferve, by afking them Queftions to anfwer filently in their own Minds, by every prudent Incitement to follow us clofely. But then we muft make them underftand, that in preaching againft Sin we never preach againft such or such a Sinner; but mean to amend and improve all, who want it: wishing every one to apply as much as possible of what he hears to his own Benefit, but nothing to the Reproach of his Neighbour.

Still you will press them in vain to pay Attention, unless you win them to it by what you have to say. And one principal Contrivance for that Purpose is to make your Sermons extremely clear. Terms and Phrases may be familiar to you, which are quite unintelligible to them: and I fear this happens much oftener than we suspect. Therefore guard against it. Your Expressions may be very common, without being low: yet employ the lowest, provided they are not ridiculous, rather than not be understood. Let your Sentences, and the Parts of them, be short, where you can. And place your Words so, especially in the longer, that your Meaning may be evident all the Way. For if they take it not immediately, they have no Time to consider of it, as they might in reading a Book: and if they are perplexed in the Beginning of a Period, they will never attempt going on with you to the End: but give

give up the Whole, as out of their Reach. Avoid Rusticity and Grossness in your Stile: yet be not too fond of smooth and soft and flowing Language; but study to be nervous and expressive; and bear the Censure of being unpolished, rather than unfluencing. Never multiply Arguments beyond Necessity; for they will only tire: abstain from weak ones; for they will discredit the strong. Employ no Arguments to prove Things, which need not be proved: for you will only make them doubtful. Employ no long or subtle Arguments to prove any Thing: but rest your Assertions on the Dictates of plain good Sense. Never express yourselves on any Point, as *having Dominion over the Faith*[d] of your Hearers; but lay before them the best Evidence, of which they are capable. In Matters too high for them, let them know, in a modest Manner, that you speak the Sentiments of the more learned, in which Providence hath by their Station directed them to acquiesce: in others, reason more at large, in the Spirit of St. *Paul*,

[d] 2 Cor. i. 24.

when

when he told the *Corinthians, I speak as to wise Men: judge ye what I say* [e].

You might perhaps give more Entertainment, and procure more Applause, by disregarding some of these Directions. But your Business is, not to please or be admired, but to do Good: to make Men think, not of your Abilities, Attainments, or Eloquence, but of the State of their own Souls; and to fix them in the Belief and Practice of what will render them happy now and to Eternity. For this Purpose (observe further) it will by no Means suffice to teach them outward Regularity and Decency; and let them fancy they have Religion enough, when they come to Church pretty constantly, and live as well as their Neighbours: though, in some Respects, ill, and, scarce in any, well, from a Principle of Conscience. Or be they from a Sense of Duty ever so honest, and sober, and chaste, and beneficent; another indispensable Part of Morals is the Discipline of the inward Man. An affectionate Piety is full as necessary, as Morals can be: and Gospel Piety no less than natural.

[e] 1 Cor. x. 15.

Here then lay your Foundation: and set before your People the lamentable Condition of fallen Man, the numerous actual Sins, by which they have made it worse, the Redemption wrought out for them by Jesus Christ, the Nature and Importance of true Faith in him, their absolute Need of the Grace of the Divine Spirit in order to obey his Precepts. This will be addressing yourselves to them as Christian Ministers ought to Christian Hearers. The holy Scriptures will furnish you with Matter for it abundantly. Short and plain Reasonings, founded on their Authority, will dart Conviction into every Mind: whereas if your Doctrine and your Speech be not that of their Bibles; if you contradict, or explain away, or pass over in Silence, any Thing taught there, they who are best contented with you, will learn little from you; and others will be offended, and quit you when they can. We have in Fact lost many of our People to Sectaries by not preaching in a Manner sufficiently evangelical: and shall neither recover them from the Extravagancies, into which they have run, nor keep more from going

going over to them, but by returning to the right Way: *declaring all the Counsel of God*[f]; and that principally, *not in the Words, which Man's Wisdom teacheth, but which the Holy Ghost teacheth*[g].

Yet the obscurer of scriptural Passages we shall do well to omit: or if there be Need, illustrate them, as far as we can, briefly: not to aim at minute Explanations of Mysteries; but urge the Belief of them from decisive Passages of God's Word, quoted according to its real Import, and leave them as that hath left them. For by attempting to throw in more Light, than our present State admits, you will only dazzle and blind those, who *saw* before as *through a Glass darkly*[h].

You are Debtors indeed *both to the wise and to the unwise*[i]. But remember, the ignorant are by far the greatest Number: and unnecessary Knowledge, if you could communicate it to them, is of small Use. But you will never be able to enlarge on abstruse and difficult Points to the Edification of the Generality: whereas you may dwell on the

[f] Acts xx. 27.   [g] 1 Cor. ii. 13.   [h] 1 Cor. xiii. 12.
[i] Rom. i. 14.

plainest to the Satisfaction and Improvement of the most learned. It is true, declining to shew Reading or Acuteness may be to some a painful Self-denial: but able Judges will easily perceive, both that you could shew them, and why you do not. Therefore enter but little, if at all, into Matters about which your Hearers are not likely to err, at least dangerously. Yet suffer not either the Evidence or the Fundamentals of Christianity, or the Honour of the Protestant Religion, or of the established Church, to want a due Support, when you are any Way called to the Defence of them. At such Times, demonstrate your Zeal; but be sure to do it with a Christian Temper; *in Meekness instructing those that oppose themselves*[k]: at others, avoid a controversial Manner, and confine yourselves to brief Instructions on these Heads.

It may possibly sometimes be necessary in our Sermons to vindicate our Rights, and *magnify our Office*[l]. But this must be done very sparingly and cautiously; so as to cut off all Pretence, that we *take the Oversight*

[k] 2. Tim. ii. 25.   [l] Rom. xi. 13.

of *God's Flock*, either *for filthy Lucre*, or from a Desire of *being Lords over his Heritage* [m]. We must never set up an undue, never a suspicious Claim: but confess, that the *Treasure* of the Gospel is committed to us entirely for the Sake of others, not our own; and that *we have it in earthen Vessels* [n]; are liable to continual Imperfections and Frailties. Such Humility is no less our Wisdom, than our Duty. For that Clergyman will always acquire the greatest Respect, who shews the most Care to deserve it, and the least Eagerness to demand it.

Every Part of your Discourses must preserve the Gravity and the Earnestness, which is inseparable from Subjects of a religious Nature. If you can speak of these lightly and negligently, your Auditors will suspect you have little Concern about them: they of Course will have less in hearing you: their Thoughts will wander to the Ends of the Earth, or their Attention to every Thing be buried in Sleep. But though languid in no Part, you will however be comparatively cool in Expositions of Scripture, in doctri-

[m] 1 Pet. v. 2, 3.   [n] 2 Cor. iv. 7.

nal, in cafuiftical Points, referving your chief Warmth for the great Articles of Chriftian Practice. There your very utmoft Endeavours will be needful to produce in your People a due Senfe of Guilt and Unworthinefs, fervent Defires of Pardon, Love to him who hath loved them, Refignation to God's Pleafure, firm Purpofes of obeying his Laws; to caution them effectually againft Profanenefs, Lukewarmnefs, Formality, Refentment, Hard-heartednefs, unjuft Love of Gain, Fondnefs of unlawful Indulgences; to infpire them with Good-will towards all Men, with proportionably kind Regards to thofe who ftand in nearer Relations to them, Diligence to be ufeful in their feveral Stations, reafonable Indifference towards the Things of this Life, pious Longings for a better. Their Degree of Knowledge, Rank and Circumftances of Life, their prevailing Notions and Cuftoms, will afford you much further Employment to make your Sermons local, if I may fo exprefs it; calculated to promote the Virtues which they are chiefly called to exercife, and guard againft the Sins of which they are chiefly in Danger. For what perfectly

fectly suits one Congregation may be extremely foreign from the Exigencies of another. And further still you must not only urge them to do their Duty, but to use the Means of doing it: which must be pointed out to them: avoiding Temptations, keeping clear of bad Company, contracting Friendships with serious and prudent Persons, employing themselves in proper Business, reading good Books, forming pious, yet prudent, Resolutions, and begging, in private Prayer, *Grace to help in Time of Need*[c]: not strictly confining their Devotions to any Forms, though Forms are very useful, but varying them according to their spiritual Condition. These are the Things, on which you must insist with your whole Force: *not as pleasing Men, but God which trieth our Hearts*[p].

Yet, while you take without Reserve all requisite Freedom, you must also take Care not to provoke, instead of reforming them; but shew, that you sincerely wish well to them; and think as well of them as you can: you must praise them when you have Opportunity; give them Cautions oftener

* Heb. iv. 16.   p 1 Thess. ii. 4.

than

than Reproofs, and never reprove harshly; but express a fatherly Concern, rather than Anger at their Faults. Represent no Fault as worse than it is: and carry no Injunction to an extravagant Height. If you do, they will either think you unreasonable, or themselves incapable of becoming good; or will run into some Absurdity by attempting it. And for their Encouragement, along with the Duties, lay before them, in a strong Light, the Comforts also, present and future, of Religion.

It is but too possible, that sometimes you must excite your People to Virtues, in which you are, more or less, deficient yourselves. For it would be heinous Unfaithfulness to omit or explain away necessary Precepts because you are imperfect in the Practice of them. And lamentable is our Case, if there be any Christian Obligation, on which we dare not for Shame speak freely: yet still worse, if we harden our Consciences, till we venture boldly to enjoin what we habitually transgress. For in that Case, not only our Credit will be utterly lost, but our Amendment almost absolutely hopeless. Therefore correct

correct your own Hearts and Lives in the first Place by the Discourses which you compose: become in all Points good Men; and then you may fearlesly speak on all Points like such.

Yet even good Men must observe a Difference. Those of less Knowledge must express themselves with less Positiveness, those of less Gravity and Discretion with less Authority and Strictness, than their Betters. And every one should consider, what his Age and Standing, Reputation for Learning, Prudence and Piety, will support him in saying; that he may not take more upon him, than will be allowed him. Yet all must assiduously take Pains to acquire, and preserve, such Esteem, that they may say with Propriety whatever their Function requires. For how unhappy would it be to disqualify yourselves from Usefulness by Levity or Indiscretion!

But even the best qualified to exhort must keep within due Bounds; convince the Judgment before they attempt to warm the Passions; rise gradually into what deserves the Name of Vehemence; and be sure neither to rife any higher, nor continue in that Strain any longer, than they are likely to carry their Auditors along with them. For if they are cold, while the Preacher is pathetic, the Impreffion made upon them will be very different from what he wifhes. And our Nation is more difpofed, than moft others, to approve a temperate Manner of fpeaking. Every Thing, which can be called Oratory, is apt to be deemed Affectation: and if it goes a great Length, raifes Contempt and Ridicule. But were the moft ferious Emotions to be raifed by mere mechanical Vehemence, they would be unfairly raifed: and what is beyond Nature will ufually foon fubfide; perhaps with Scorn, upon Reflection, of what was admired when heard. Or fuppofing fuch Admiration to continue, bad Effects may as poffibly follow as good: whereas Warmth of Affection, excited to a proper Degree by the rational Enforcement of folid Arguments, promifes to be durable, and will never do Harm. The Faculty of moving Hearers thus, is a moft valuable Bleffing. And fuch as have but little of it, may confiderably improve it, by labouring

labouring to affect themselves deeply with what they would say; and thinking, what Methods of saying it will be most persuasive. But they must not attempt to force an unwilling Genius too far. If they do, what it produces will be so ungraceful and unsuccessful, that they had much better content themselves to do as well as they can in their own Way.

Your Delivery must in the first Place be such, that you can be heard; else you preach in vain: besides that speaking too low argues Indolence and Indifference; whereas an audible Exertion is a Mark of Earnestness: and the common People are peculiarly pleased, when their Minister appears to take Pains about them. But then you must neither be precipitately quick, (for if your Words be understood, your Meaning will not) nor tediously slow; nor sink any one Part of your Sentence under its proper Level, especially the concluding Part. Distinctness will do much to supply Want of Strength in speaking: which however it is very material that you should try to remedy gradually, as many have done, by a prudent Exercise of

your

your Voice. Yet ſtraining beyond your due Pitch will give your Hearers Pain, make you in ſome Degree inarticulate, and produce a ſinging Sort of Cadence and Tone. This laſt indeed hath been ſometimes known to pleaſe weak Perſons: but it cannot poſſibly make them either wiſer or better: and it offends the judicious extremely. Many learn in their Childhood a provincial Dialect, which they cannot lay aſide eaſily; and yet ſhould endeavour it, eſpecially if they ſettle in a different Part of the Nation. Some acquire uncouth Accents one knows not how: ſome bring them from the School or the College: and now and then one ſeems to hear a theatrical Pronunciation; which hath been condemned even by Heathen Writers upon Oratory; and is the very worſt, that a Chriſtian Orator can adopt. It reminds his Hearers, greatly to his Diſcredit, where he muſt probably have learnt it: he will alſo appear by Means of it to be only acting a Part, and be regarded accordingly. Indeed all remarkable Imitation, in Delivery as well as Compoſition, though of a Perſon in your own Profeſſion, and one juſtly admired,

mired, will be disliked. You will never attain to any advantageous Resemblance of his Manner: but, by a mistaken or overdone Mimicry, turn what may perhaps be graceful in the Original, into Oddness. Or could you avoid that, you would lessen your Weight and Influence: which must arise from speaking in your own Character, not personating another. Every Man's Voice and Utterance, as well as his Face, belongs to himself alone; and it is vain to think either of looking or talking like such or such a one. Therefore preserve what is native to you: free it from adventitious Faults: improve it, if you can: but remember, that you may deprave it by the Endeavour; and certainly will, if you change it essentially. Speak to your People, as you would in Conversation, when you undertake to inform or persuade a Friend, in a Concern of great Moment; only with more Deliberateness, more Strength and Energy, in Proportion to the Numbers: and vary both your Stile and your Elocution, as in Conversation you always do, suitably to your Matter. For Monotony both absolutely prevents Emotion, and soon deadens Attention.

Attention. It is worst indeed, when uniformly unnatural, by degenerating into a kind of Chant. But merely to be uniformly inexpreſſive, be it through Heavineſs, or Effeminacy, or inſignificant Lightneſs, is either very blameable, or, if it cannot be helped, very unhappy. And perhaps, a little even of injudicious Variety is better than a weariſome Sameneſs.

In public ſpeaking, Perſons commonly fall into Errors, and ſometimes great ones, without perceiving it, though they can obſerve ſmall ones in others. Therefore you will act prudently in deſiring ſome Wellwiſher, on whoſe Judgment and Frankneſs you can depend, to advertiſe you of any Thing wrong in the Conduct of your Voice, or in your Action; and you will ſhew your Gratitude and good Senſe by ſtudying to amend it.

We of this Nation are not given to uſe or to admire much Action, either in ordinary Diſcourſe, or even in popular Harangues. And, were it for this Reaſon only, a Preacher ſhould be moderate in it. But beſides, in the Nature of the Thing, you had far better have none, than what is unbecoming, or unmeaning, or unsuitable to what you are saying, or repeated at certain Distances, whatever you are saying. Yet somewhat of Gesture, appearing to be artless, and regulated by Propriety, may be very useful, especially in the warmer Parts, of Exhortation, Reproof, or even Argument. For to be altogether motionless, when the Subject is animating, and our Language perhaps vehement, seems an Inconsistency; and may raise a Doubt, whether we are in earnest. But still Defect in Action is better than Excess. And a great deal cannot well be used by those who read their Sermons.

This is one Objection against reading them: and there are several besides. Persons, who are short-sighted, have peculiar Reasons to avoid it. Indeed almost all Persons are accustomed from their early Years to read in a different Tone, from that in which they read at other Times: and we seldom correct it throughly. Or if we did, what we say in such Manner as to make it seem the present Dictate of our own Hearts, will much better make its Way into the Hearts of others, than

than if our Eyes are fixed all the while on a Paper, from which we visibly recite the Whole. It will ordinarily be uttered too with more disengaged Freedom and livelier Spirit. The Preacher also will be abler to enforce his Words by significant Looks: to perceive from the Countenances of his Hearers, what they comprehend, and by what they are moved: and may accordingly enlarge on that Head, or proceed to another, as he finds Cause. He may likewise oppose with Success irregular itinerant Declaimers, who affect and gain Popularity by this Method: and as their credulous Followers are apt to think it a supernatural Gift, he may undeceive them, by imitating in this Case the Practice of St. *Paul* in another, which he describes thus: *what I do, that I will do; that wherein they glory, they may be found even as we* [q]. But then there must be a long and diligent Preparation to do this well: some will scarce ever attain sufficient Presence of Mind, and Readiness of Expression: others will acquit themselves handsomely in a good Flow of Spirits, but meanly when these fail them:

[q] 2 Cor. xi. 12.

and

and though little Inaccuracies will be observed by few, yet Hesitations will by all, and every other considerable Fault by sensible Hearers, to the Preacher's great Disgrace. Or if such do get the Faculty of being always able to say something plausible, it will tempt them to neglect the Improvement of their Understandings and their Discourses; and to be content with digressing, whenever they are at a Loss, from their Text and their Subject, to any Point, on which they can be copious: to utter off Hand such Crudities, as they could not bear to write down; and think the meanest of extempore Effusions good enough for the Populace. Now on the contrary, previously studying and writing Sermons tends to fill them with well digested and well adapted Matter, disposed in right Order: especially, if you will carefully revise them every Time you preach them; supply Deficiencies, blot out Repetitions, correct Improprieties, guard against Misapprehensions, enlighten what is obscure, familiarize what is too high, transpose what is wrongly placed, strengthen the weak Parts, animate the languid ones. Your Composition needs not be be at all the ftiffer, but may be the freer, for the Pains thus employed upon it. You may frame it purpofely to be fpoken as if you were not reading it: and by looking it over a few Times when you are about to ufe it, you may deliver it almoft without being obferved to read it. The more you acquire of this Art, the more you will be liked, and the ftronger Impreffion you will make: But after all, *every Man*, as the Apoftle faith on a different Occafion, *hath his proper Gift of God; one after this Manner, another after that* [r]: let each cultivate his own; and no one cenfure or defpife his Brother. There is a middle Way, ufed by our Predeceffors, of fetting down, in fhort Notes, the Method and principal Heads, and enlarging on them in fuch Words as prefent themfelves at the Time. Perhaps, duly managed, this would be the beft. That which is, or lately was, common amongft foreign Divines, of writing Sermons firft, then getting and repeating them by Heart, not only is unreafonably laborious, but fubjects Perfons to the Hazard of ftopping difagreeably, and even breaking

[r] 1 Cor. vii. 7.

off

off abruptly, for want of Memory. Or if they escape that Danger, there still remains another, of saying their Lesson with ungraceful Marks of Fear and Caution.

Instead of taking a Text, which comprehends within itself the whole Subject, of which you would treat, it may often be useful to chuse one, which hath a Reference to Things preceding and following it, and to expound all the Context. This will afford you a Variety of Matter, and give you Opportunities for short unexpected Remarks; with which Persons are frequently more struck, than with an entire Discourse; for of the latter they foresee the Drift all the Way, and therefore set themselves to fence against it. Thus also you may illustrate the Beauties, at the same Time that you shew the practical Uses, of large Portions of Scripture at once: for Instance, of a Parable, a Conversation, a Miracle of our blessed Lord; or a Narration concerning this or that other memorable Person, whether deserving of Praise or Blame. For Scripture Histories and Examples are easily remembered, and have great Weight. In Proportion as we overlook them, we shall appear

appear less to be Ministers of God's Word: and our People will have less Veneration for us, or for it, or for both. You may also in this Method, as you go along, obviate Objections to Passages of God's Word without stating them in Form, at which otherwise many may stumble, if they read with Attention: and if they do not attend, they will read with no Profit. Several Things in holy Writ seem to be strange; hardly consistent one with another, or with our natural Notions. Of these Difficulties, which must always perplex Persons, and may often deliver them over a Prey to Infidels, you may occasionally remove one and another; meddling with none, but such as you can overcome: and from your Success in these, you may observe to your Auditors the Probability, that others are capable of Solutions also. Perhaps they will forget your Solution: but they will remember that they heard one, and may have it repeated to them, if they please. By these Means you will teach your People, what is grievously wanting in the present Age, to value their Bibles more, and understand them better: and to read them both with Pleasure and

and Profit, drawing from them useful Inferences and Observations, as they have heard you do. Formerly Courses of Lectures on whole Books of Scripture were customary in Churches; and they were doubtless extremely beneficial. It would not be easy, if possible, to revive these now: but the Practice, which I have been proposing to you, is some Approach towards them.

I would also advise you to instruct your Parishioners, amongst other Things, from some proper Text or Texts, in the daily and occasional Services of the Church: not with a View to extol either immoderately, much less to provoke Wrath against those who dissent from us; but mildly to answer unjust Imputations upon our Liturgy, and chiefly to shew the Meaning, the Reasons, the Uses of each Part; that your Congregations may, as the Apostle expresses it, *pray with the Understanding* [s]. In all Compositions, there will be some Things, which to some Persons want explaining: and, were the Whole ever so clear, Men are strangely apt both to hear and to speak Words, that are become familiar to

[s] 1 Cor. xiv. 15.

them, with scarce any Attention to their Sense. And so by Degrees a bodily Attendance and Worship becomes all that they pay: and they return Home almost as little edified, as they would by Devotions in a Tongue unknown. Convincing them of this Fault, and assisting them to amend it, must greatly contribute to the Promotion of true Piety amongst them. Nor will it be a small Benefit, if, in the Course of your liturgical Instructions, you can persuade the Bulk of your Congregations to join in the decent Use of Psalmody, as their Forefathers did; instead of the present shameful Neglect of it, by almost all, and the conceited Abuse of it by a few.

But a fervent Desire of being useful will teach you more than any particular Directions can, upon every Head. Without this Desire, you will either be negligent; or if you would seem zealous, you will be detected for Want of Uniformity and Perseverance. Therefore make sure first that all be right within, and *out of the good Treasure of the Heart you will bring forth good Things*[t], naturally and pru-

[t] Matth. xii. 35.

dently, and, through the Grace of the Holy Spirit, effectually. It is not easy indeed even to instruct the willing; much less to convince the unwilling, and reform the wicked. But still these are the Purposes, for which we are God's Embassadors: and we must try with indefatigable Perseverance every Way to execute our Commission. We must study human Nature in our own Breasts, and those of others: we must acquaint ourselves, by all innocent Means, with the Opinions and Practices of the World, especially of our Hearers, that we may lay their Hearts and Lives open to their View, and make them feel what we say. We must consider all the while we compose, and reconsider as we preach and afterwards: " Is this adapted " sufficiently to the Capacities, the State of " Mind, the Circumstances of the poor " People who are to hear it: will this Part " be clear, that home enough, a third well " guarded against Mistakes: will they go " back as much better disposed than they " came, as it is in our Power to make them?" Perhaps one or more Ways of representing a necessary Doctrine or Duty have failed. We must

must think, whether a more likely may not be found, or a less likely in Appearance prove more successful.

If you have preached a considerable Time in a Place, and done little or no Good; there must in all Probability, be some Fault, not only in your Hearers, but in you or your Sermons. *For the Word of God*, when duly dispensed, is to this Day, as it was originally, *powerful, and sharper than a two-edged Sword*[u]. Inquire then, where the Fault may be. Never despair, nor be immoderately grieved, if your Success be small: but be not indifferent about it: do not content yourselves with the indolent Plea, that you have done your Duty, and are not answerable for the Event. You may have done it as far as the Law requires: yet by no Means have discharged your Consciences. You may have done it conscientiously, yet not with the Diligence or the Address that you ought. And as we are seldom easy in other Cases, when we fail of our End; if we are so in this, it doth not look well. At least consult

[u] Heb. iv. 12.

your Hearts upon the Point. And if you have been deficient, beg of God Pardon, Grace and Direction; endeavour to do more for your People; consult your Brethren about the Means. Conversation of this Nature will much better become Clergymen when they meet, than any which is not relative to their Profession, or only relative to the Profits of it. But especially ask the Advice of the most able and serious.

I am very sensible, that in all the Particulars before-mentioned I have been far from observing sufficiently myself the Rules which I have now recommended to you: but hope I shall make some Amends, though late, to the Church of Christ, by exhorting and directing others. It was my Purpose, after speaking of stated Instructions, to have proceeded to occasional ones: a very important and sadly neglected Part of the pastoral Care. But my Strength will not suffice: and I have detained you already too long. If God spare me to another like Occasion, that shall be my Subject. If not, as is most probable,

probable, I shall endeavour to leave behind me some Admonitions to you concerning it [w]. At present I can only intreat you to consider very seriously, what Numbers there are in most Parishes, and therefore perhaps in yours; whom you cannot think to be in a State of Salvation; and how greatly it imports you to use with them, as you solemnly promised at your Ordination, not only *public* but *private Monitions, as Need shall require, and Occasion shall be given.* The eternal Welfare of many poor Creatures may depend on this: and your own is deeply concerned in it, as God himself hath declared: who will certainly expect that what he requires you to do, be done to the very utmost of your Ability. *Son of Man, I have made thee a Watchman unto the House of Israel: therefore hear the Word at my Mouth, and give them Warning from me. If thou dost not speak to warn the wicked from his wicked Way, he shall die in his Iniquity, but his blood will I require at thine Hand.*

---

[w] Nothing of this Kind has been found among his Grace's Papers.

But if thou warn the wicked, and he turn not from his Wickedness, he shall die in his Iniquity, but thou hast delivered thy Soul [x].

[x] Ezek. iii. 17, 18, 19, xxxiii. 7, 8, 9.

INSTRUCTIONS

INSTRUCTIONS

GIVEN TO

CANDIDATES

FOR

ORDERS

After their subscribing the ARTICLES.

Gentlemen,

YOU have now made the Subscription, by Law required. And as, in so doing, you have acknowledged the Liturgy and Articles of the Church of *England* to be agreeable to the Word of God; I hope you will think yourselves bound, as you are, to be careful, that the Instructions which you give, and the Doctrines which you maintain, in public and in private, be agreeable to that Liturgy and those Articles: that you neither contradict, nor omit to inculcate and defend, on proper Occasions, the Truths, which they contain.

In the next Place I exhort you to spend a due Share of the Remainder of this Day in what, I trust, hath employed not a little of your Time already; weighing diligently the

Nature and Importance of the Undertaking, in which you are about to engage; forming suitable Resolutions; and earnestly begging that Grace of God, which alone can *make you able Ministers of the New Testament* [a].

Nothing is better fitted to assist you in this good Work, than the Office of Ordination, of Deacons or Priests, as you are respectively concerned. You must certainly have read it over, before you offered yourselves. Since that, you have been directed to read it again. But I desire you to peruse it once more this Afternoon with your best Attention, that you may join in it tomorrow with a greater degree of rational Seriousness; and particularly, that you may answer, on more deliberate Consideration, the Questions, which will then be put to you. For there can hardly be a Case, in which either Insincerity, or even Thoughtlessness, would carry in it heavier Guilt.

And that you may be in no Perplexity concerning the Meaning or Fitness of any Part of the Office, it may be useful to go through some Parts of it along with you

[a] 2 Cor. iii. 6.

beforehand,

beforehand, proceeding as they lie in the Book.

The first Thing, which Candidates, both for Deacons and Priests Orders, after they are presented, are required to do, as distinct from the rest of the Congregation, is to take the Oaths of Allegiance, and Supremacy: For as you are to be Ministers of the Church established by Law in this Nation, it is evidently reasonable, that the civil Government, established by Law, should be assured of the Fidelity and Affection of Persons to whom it gives and secures Privileges and Profits; and who are intrusted with the Care, amongst other Matters, of making Men good Subjects. Now these Oaths bind every Person, who takes them, to *honour the King* [b], and by Consequence all that are put in Authority under him, both in Word and Deed; and to *lead*, in Subjection to them, *quiet and peaceable Lives* [c]. That these Things may with a good Conscience be promised and performed, there is no just Cause of Doubt. But if any one thinks there is, he ought to apply for Satisfaction:

[b] 1 Pet. ii. 17.   [c] 1 Tim. ii. 2.

and

and till he receives it, he ought to abstain from taking the Oaths. *For whatever is not of Faith, is Sin*[d]: and in this Case it would be no less, than Perjury. Nothing is a Plea sufficient for committing any Sin, much less one so heinous: not even all the Force, that can be used. But here is no Shadow of Force. You are come voluntarily to offer yourselves, well knowing that the Oaths must be tendered to you: that is, you have made it your Choice to take them.

But by your Subscription you have entered into a further Obligation: to use the Liturgy in all your public Ministrations[e]: and therefore, to pray for the King by Name, for his long Life and Prosperity, for his obtaining Victory over all his Enemies. God forbid, that any one, who doth this, should be disaffected to the Government, under which we live. And if we are Friends, it is both our Duty and our Wisdom to shew that we are. For thus we shall strengthen an Establishment, on which, under God, the safe Enjoyment of our Religion intirely depends; we shall procure the Support, which we

[d] Rom. xiv. 23. [e] Can. 36.

cannot but be senfible, that we want; and we shall silence, or at least confute those, who love to speak despitefully against us on this Head.

After the Oaths, Candidates for Deacons Orders are asked: *Do you trust that you are inwardly moved by the Holy Ghost to take upon you this Office and Ministration?* A solemn Question: and which ought to be well considered, before it is answered. Observe then: it is not said, *Do you feel*; have you an immediate Perception of such an Impulse from the Holy Ghost, as you can distinguish from all other inward Movements by its Manner of impressing you: but, *Do you trust*; are you on good Grounds persuaded? What then are the proper Grounds of such Persuasion?

In the first Place, if he hath not moved you effectually to live *soberly, righteously, and godly* [f], you may be sure he hath not moved you to assume the Office of a Minister in God's Church. Examine yourselves therefore strictly on this Point: a most important one to all Men; but to you, if possible,

[f] Tit. ii. 12.

above

above all: and before you presume to officiate in his House, ask your Hearts, Do you transgress, do you omit, no Duty, wilfully or knowingly? Have you a genuine practical Faith in Christ? Are you, on the Terms of the Gospel Covenant, intitled to everlasting Life? But supposing that you are, more is requisite in the present Case: and what more, the latter Part of the Question points out. *To serve God, for the promoting of his Glory, and the edifying of his Church.* This then being the Design of the Office; if, so far as you know your own Hearts, this is your Motive to desire it; and if, so far as you can judge of your own Abilities and Attainments, they are equal to it in some competent Degree: then you may safely answer, that *you trust you are moved by the Holy Ghost to take it upon you.* For *we* can *have such Trust to Godward* only *through Christ,* who hath sent us the Spirit: *we are not sufficient to* do or *think any Thing as of ourselves: but our Sufficiency is of God*[g]. Together with this principal Motive, of *serving God* by *edifying his People,*

[g] 2 Cor. iii. 4, 5.

you may allowably have the subordinate one, of providing a decent Maintenance for your own Support, and for those who may belong to you: but if you are indifferent or cool about the former, and attentive only or chiefly to the latter: since you cannot think that such Dispositions are approved by the Holy Spirit, as proper for the Ministry, you will be guilty of *lying to him*[h], if you affirm, that he hath moved you to enter on it with them. Therefore inspect your Souls thoroughly; and form them, by the Help of divine Grace, to be duly influenced by the right Principle, before you venture to answer this Question: which is very wisely made the leading one; because your Inducement will be the Rule of your Behaviour, and probably also the Measure of your Success.

The next Question, put to those who apply for Deacons Orders, and the first to such as have received them, and desire to be admitted Priests, is, *Do you think, that you are truly called, according to the Will of Christ, and the due Order of this Realm, to the Ministry of the Church?* This is, are you con-

[h] Acts v. 3.

scious

scious neither of any Defect in Body or Mind, nor of any other Impediment, which may, for the present, if not for ever, be, according to the Laws of God or Man, a just Obstacle in your Way? Such Things may escape our Knowledge or Memory. Therefore we call upon you to inform us. And you are bound to answer with Sincerity.

It is not requisite, that I should enlarge on every Question; though it is, that you should weigh every one seriously. That, which recites the Duties of Deacons, may seem to have some Difficulty in it: as it assigns to them Occupations, which the Acts of the Apostles do not, in the History of their Appointment[1]; and as they are but little employed now in the single Business, there allotted to them. But that Passage of Scripture plainly was intended to set forth, only the immediate and urgent Reason of ordaining them, not the Whole of what was, then or soon after, given them in Charge. For we find in the same Book, that *Philip* the Deacon both preached and baptized[k]. And the Qualifications, required in Deacons

[1] Acts vi.   [k] Acts viii. 5—13, 26—40.

by

by St. *Paul* [l], intimate very clearly, that more Things muſt, even then, have been incumbent upon them, than adminiſtering to the Relief of the Poor. Accordingly, from the primitive Ages downwards, they are deſcribed as performing occaſionally moſt of the ſame Offices, which they do now; and being, what their Name denotes, aſſiſtant and ſubſervient to Prieſts in all proper Employments [m]. And the leſs they are engaged in their chief original one, the more Opportunity and the more Need they have, to ſhew Diligence in the other good Works, belonging or ſuited peculiarly to their Station.

The next Queſtion is common to Candidates for each Order: *Will you faſhion your own Lives, and thoſe of your Families, ſo far as in you lieth, to be wholeſome Examples to the Flock of Chriſt?* This extends to avoiding in your own Behaviour, and reſtraining in theirs, Follies, Levities, mean and diſreputable Actions, as well as Crimes and Vices. The Apoſtle enjoins *Deacons and their Wives to be grave* [n]: much more than ought Prieſts.

[l] 1 Tim. iii. 8—13.   [m] See *Bingham's* Orig. Eccl. l. 2. c. 20.   [n] 1 Tim. iii. 8, 11.

He enjoins every Christian to *abstain from all Appearance of Evil*[o]. And our blessed Lord enjoins all his Disciples to *be wise*, as well as *harmless*[p]. Therefore govern yourselves and yours by these Rules: and consider frequently, whether you observe them well. For without it you will neither gain Esteem, nor do good.

The last Question, put alike to the whole Number of Candidates, is, *Will you reverently obey your Ordinary, and them to whom the Government over you is committed?* You would be bound to this, though you were not to promise it: for both Reason and Scripture demand it. Still more firmly you will be bound, when you have promised it, though it were of small Importance. But it is of very great, not only to the Dignity and Ease of your Superiors, but to your own Interest, and the Benefit of the whole Church. Our Saviour both commands, and prayed for Unity amongst his Followers in the most expressive Terms[q]. Without Union there cannot be a sufficient Degree either of Strength

---

[o] 1 Thess. v. 22.　[p] Matth. x. 16.　[q] John xiii. 34, 35. xvii. 11, 12, 21, 22, 23.

or Beauty: and without Subordination there cannot long be Union. Therefore *obey*, as the Apostle directs, *them that have the Rule over you* [r]; and promote their Honour, their Credit, their Influence. This will make us abler to serve the Cause of Religion, and protect you. And God forbid that, so far as we are able, we should ever fail to be willing and zealous.

In the Office for the Ordination of Priests, after a pious and awful Charge, which I recommend to your most serious Attention, follow several Questions of the greatest Moment, your Answers to which, I hope, you will remember to the last Day of your Lives. In these Answers, besides what hath been already mentioned, you promise, that *the Doctrine and Discipline of Christ, as contained in Scripture, and received in this Church and Realm*, shall be the Standard of your teaching and acting; and every Thing contrary to them be faithfully opposed by you: that you will *use both public and private Monitions and Exhortations, as well to the Sick as to the Whole, within your Cures*; and that, as fre-

[r] Heb. xiii. 17.

quently and fully *as Need shall require, and Occasion be given.* You promise also, that *you will be diligent in Prayers and reading the Holy Scriptures;* which by the preceding Exhortation evidently appears to mean, private Prayer and Reading; *and in such Studies, as help to the Knowledge of Scripture; laying aside the Study of the World and the Flesh*: that is, not making, either gross Pleasures, or more refined Amusements, even literary ones unconnected with your Profession, or Power, or Profit, or Advancement, or Applause, your great Aim in Life; but labouring chiefly to qualify yourselves for doing Good to the Souls of Men, and applying carefully to that Purpose whatever Qualifications you attain. Further yet, you promise, that *you will maintain and set forwards, as much as lieth in you, Quietness, Peace and Love among all Christian People;* and *especially among them, that are or shall be committed to your Charge.* By this you oblige yourselves, never to raise or promote personal, family, parochial, ecclesiastical, political, or any other, Animosities; but to discourage, and, if possible, compose and extinguish them; than which

which you cannot perform a more Chriſtian Part, or one more conducive to your Honour and your Uſefulneſs.

But, beſides pondering well beforehand theſe Anſwers, which you are to make, I earneſtly beg you, to read and think them over often afterwards: and particularly, at each Return of the Ember Weeks to examine yourſelves, as in the Preſence of God, whether you have made good the Engagement, into which you entered at your Ordination. So far as you have, this Practice will afford you the greateſt poſſible Comfort : ſo far as you may have failed, it will ſuggeſt to you the moſt uſeful Admonition.

After theſe Queſtions, a ſhort Silence is appointed to be kept for the ſecret Prayers of the Congregation, that God would enable and incline you to do what you have undertaken: which Bleſſing, I hope, you will aſk at the ſame Time for yourſelves very earneſtly. Then follows a Hymn of conſiderable Antiquity: and to be repeated with much Reverence, on Account of the important Petitions and Doctrines comprized in it, though it be altogether void of Ornament in that old Tran-

ſlation,

flation, which we still retain. Next to this, follows a very proper Address to the Throne of Grace, pronounced by the Bishop alone, in the Name of the whole Assembly: which is instantly succeeded by the Act of Ordination.

The first Words of that, *Receive the Holy Ghost*, were used by our Saviour to his Apostles, immediately after he had said, *as my Father hath sent me, even so send I you*[s]. God gave not the Spirit by Measure unto him[t]: and he was able to bestow what Measure he pleased, both of spiritual Gifts and Graces, upon others. He meant however by this Benediction to confer only the ordinary ones: for the extraordinary, you know, were reserved till after his Ascension. Far be it from the Bishops of his Church to claim, even in Respect of the former, the Powers which he had. But still these Words in our Mouths, when spoken over you, properly express, in the first Place, the Communication of that Authority, which proceeds from the Holy Ghost. For we read, that *the Holy Ghost said, Separate me Barnabas and Saul for*

[s] John xx. 21, 22. [t] John iii. 34.

the Work, whereunto I have called them[u]: and that the latter of these exhorted the Elders of the Church of *Ephesus, Take Heed to the Flock, over which the Holy Ghost hath made you Overseers*[w]. They also express, in the second Place, our earnest request to the Father of Mercies, that you may at all Times enjoy such Proportions, both of the Graces and Gifts of the Spirit, as will be needful for you: which Request, if it be not your own Fault, will prove effectual; because having, in the common Course of his Providence, appointed us, though unworthy, to act in this Behalf, he will assuredly be ready to own and bless our Ministrations.

It follows very soon: *whose Sins thou dost forgive, they are forgiven; and whose Sins thou dost retain, they are retained.* These again are the Words of Christ to his Apostles, immediately after the former. But he did not grant to them the Power, either of retaining the Sins of penitent Persons, or of forgiving the impenitent. Nor do we pretend to grant, by uttering them, all the Powers, which the Apostles had in this

[u] Acts xiii. 2. [w] Acts xx. 28.

Respect. They had *the Discernment of Spirits*[x]: and could say with Certainty, when Persons were penitent, and consequently forgiven, and when not[y]. They were able also to inflict miraculous punishments on Offenders; and to remove, on their Repentance, the Punishments, which had been inflicted. These Words will convey Nothing of all this to you. But still, when we use them, they give you, first, an Assurance, that according to the Terms of that Gospel, which you are to preach, Men shall be pardoned or condemned: secondly, a Right of inflicting ecclesiastical Censures for a shorter or longer Time, and of taking them off; which, in Regard to external Communion, is retaining or forgiving Offences. This Power, being bestowed for the Edification of the Church, must be restrained, not only by general Rules of Order, but according to the particular Exigencies of Circumstances. And our Church Wishes, with much Reason, for Circumstances more favourable to the Exertion of it[z]. But how little soever exerted,

[x] 1 Cor. xii. 10. [y] Acts viii. 21, 23. of Commination. [z] Office

the Power is inherent in the Office of Priesthood. And though we are no more infallible in our Proceedings and Sentences, than temporal Judges are in theirs; yet our Acts, as well as theirs, are to be respected, as done by competent Authority. And if they are done on good Grounds also, *whatever we shall bind or loose on Earth, will be bound or loosed in Heaven*[a]. Nor will other Proofs of Repentance be sufficient in the Sight of God, if Submission to the Discipline of the Church of Christ, when it hath been offended, and requires due Satisfaction, be obstinately refused, either from Haughtiness or Negligence.

To these Words is subjoined the concluding Charge: *and be thou a faithful Dispenser of the Word of God, and of his holy Sacraments.* This then is the Stewardship committed to you. And you cannot but see, in what a profane and corrupt Age it is committed to you: how grievously Religion, and its Ministers, are hated or despised; how lamentably both they, and its other Professors, are degenerated and divided. Your Business

[a] Matth. xviii. 18.

will be, each within the Sphere of his Influence, to prevent thefe Things from growing worfe; which, bad as they are, they ftill may; and, if poffible, to make them better; or at leaft, to recover or preferve fuch, as you can, from the general Depravity. But you will never fucceed in your Attempts for this Purpofe, either by Bitternefs againft Infidels, Heretics, and Sectaries, or by Contempt and Ridicule of enthufiaftic or fuperftitious Perfons. The only right Method is a very different one: diligent Study, to fit yourfelves more completely for teaching and vindicating the Truths of Chriftianity: fcriptural and rational Inftruction, affiduoufly given, with Zeal and Mildnefs duly tempered, and fuited to the Capacities and Condition of your Hearers: a willing and devout and affecting Performance of all facred Rites, whether in the Church or elfewhere: but above all, a Behaviour, innocent, humble, peaceable, difinterefted, beneficent, abftemious, difcreet, religious.

Take Heed therefore to your Steps: and walk in the prefent evil Days with fuch Piety and Caution, that, as the Office exhorts,

you

you may neither offend, nor be Occasion that others offend; but may *cut off Occasion from them which desire Occasion* [b] against you; that *they who are of the contrary Part, and falsely accuse your good Converfation in Chrift, may be ashamed*[c] of themselves; or however, that your Master and Judge may not *be ashamed of you*[d] at the great Day, but pronounce over each of you, *Well done, good and faithful Servant; enter thou into the Joy of thy Lord*[e].

[b] 2 Cor. xi. 12. [c] Tit. ii. 8. 1 Pet. iii. 16. [d] Mark viii. 38. Luke ix. 26. [e] Matth. xxv. 21.

ORATIO

quam coram

SYNODO

PROVINCIÆ CANTUARIENSIS

Anno 1761 convocatâ

habendam fcripferat,

fed morbo præpeditus non habuit,

ARCHIEPISCOPUS,

SAtisfecistis egregie, Fratres, nostræ omnium expectationi, Prolocutore electo, quem naturæ dotibus cumulatum, fide Christiana penitus imbutum, humanitate politum, eruditione excultum, auctoritate gravem novimus: atque adeo dignissimum, qui a viro laudato iis ornaretur præconiis, quæ in utrumque conveniunt. Concesso igitur vobis libenter, quem petitis, Referendario, intendamus jam communiter animos in ea, quæ hodiernæ celebritatis ratio postulat. Et hæc quidem, licet minime idoneus, tamen cum id sit officii mei, conabor exponere; oratione usus Latinâ, (sic enim est in more positum, nequid, puto, intelligant inepti auditores) nulla autem adhibita dicendi elegantia; quam si sectarer tandem post quadraginta ferme annorum desuetudinem, omnino non assequerer; sed familiari admodum ac tenui sermone: Deum orans ut quod
e pectore

e pectore meo proveniet in vestra descendat, et fructum ferat. Neque enim plausum, ne vestrum quidem, capto; de hoc unice sollicitus, ut aliquid, si possum, proferam, quo sapientiores et meliores utrinque evadamus, et servi fideles utilesque domini nostri Jesu Christi inveniamur in supremo illo die.

Convenimus, Patres Fratresque, in id parati, ut opem feramus veræ religioni, bonisque moribus, modo quidpiam ejusmodi nobis demandetur. Quod cum jam diu non sit factum, rogitant homines procacioris ingenii, quorsum huc ridenda solennitate, sic enim interpretantur, congregamur, quibus nihil negotii datum est, nec etiam dabitur. Sinite quæso, ut huic petulantiæ, nimium grassanti, pauca prius reponam, quam ad alia progrediar.

Illudne ergo spernendum existimant, quod hæc sacra Synodus eodem antiquissimo jure constituta est, quo comitia procerum & eorum qui plebis vicem gerunt; quodque optimi Principis jussu acciti comparemus? Reverebuntur, qui recta sapiunt, utramque partem, tam ecclesiasticam quam civilem, reipublicæ Britannicæ, nec vel unum lapidem,
præsertim

præsertim qui fundamenta contingat, ex venerando ædificio dimotum cupient, ne totius molis, ut superiore sæculo, ruina consequatur. Multa fecit hic cœtus in redintegranda puriori fide cultuque, reipublicæ cumprimis utilia: hoc solo meritus, ut semper in posterum honorifice convocaretur. Quæ porro sit facturus, vel nunc vel posthac, quandocunque concessa fuerit aliquid agendi facultas, in pejus præjudicari non debet: neque paulo modestiores negaturos putem, quin ab eo non pauca in commune bonum fieri possent, et a nobis fierent lubenter. Quid quod & interim orientur ab hoc consessu commoda non mediocria? Videbunt cives nostri in eum intuentes, quinam simus, qui ecclesiæ Anglicanæ, Episcopi, Decani, Archidiaconi, præsidemus; qualesque sibi delegerit Procuratores Clerus parochialis: unde fore confidimus, ut nihil sibi a nobis extimescendum esse autument, sed omnia quæ bona sunt speranda. Congregati preces coram Deo fudimus concorditer: quas quin ille, promissi memor, clementer acceperit, nefas est dubitare. Hortationi interfuistis, pietate pariter ac prudentia summa refertæ, quæ etsi multorum aures recitata prætervolaverit,

prætervolaverit, omnium animos lecta inflammabit. Consilia etiam saluberima præsentes invicem pro re nata communicabimus. Licebit denique Regem uno ore suppliciter compellare; nostram in illum fidem & observantiam, in religionem, virtutem, legitimam libertatem, cum civilem tum ecclesiasticam, studium testari; eoque efficere, ut etiamsi natura atque institutione nunquam non fuerit præconibus veritatis propitius, fiat tamen indies benignior, & spretis male feriatorum hominum cavillationibus, quicquid vel factu vel creditu indignum est, cohibeat, quantum salva unicuique conscientiæ prærogativa potest; *quæcunque* autem sunt *vera, quæcunque pudica, justa, sancta, amabilia, bonæ, formæ*[a], non solum, ut semper, exemplo, sed monitis privatim, edictis publice, animose tueatur.

Hæc nihil esse, nemo dixerit: satis non esse, ultro fateor. Disquiramus igitur, unde quod deest possit accedere.

Clamabunt extemplo fervidiores, argumentis, obtestationibus, amicorum deprecatione, purpuratorum gratia, omni machina

[a] Phil. iv. 8.

contendendum,

contendendum, ut quæcunque jura Synodis prioribus fuerunt attributa, iifdem armetur et hæc, regio mandato: refufcitandam demum ejus ope collapfam & emortuam veteris Ecclefiæ difciplinam, atque exercendam ftrenue; noftrâ enim nos jam pridem eviluiffe inertia. Et hi quidem plerumque religiofi funt viri, multaque lectione exercitati. Sed parum vident, quid ferant tempora, quove loco fimus.

Primum adverfarios habemus omnes, non modo qui Deum effe aperte negant, quos omni tempore fuiffe paucos arbitror, fed eos etiam qui, ut ifte olim, *oratione relinquunt, re tollunt:* & fub recenti latitantes Deiftarum nomine, fi verum eloqui oportet, Athei funt. Neque enim numen illud fuum bonos remunerari, neque improbos punire credunt: unde nullius foret momenti, exifteret necne. Proinde conftant in eo fibi quod nullum ei honorem, vel una vel fcorfim, quantum ego quidem inaudiverim, exhibeant; & naturæ, quas vocant, leges iis limitibus quifque circumfcribat, qui lubidini fuæ optime congruant; eæque forte mutata, confeftim aliud fibi juris naturalis corpus effingant, vel exceptiones quafdam futiles in fui gratiam excogitent,

excogitent, ut permiſſum videatur quicquid arridet. Licentiam interim, quam ſibi infinitam aſſerunt, adeo gravate cum piis communicant, ut a cultu divino quoſlibet obvios ſanniis & convitiis arceant, ſuos vero nonnunquam interdictionibus minisſque; egregii ſcilicet, immo vero, ſi creditis, unici, libertatis vindices.

Cum his fere ſe conjungunt, neque multo ſunt nobis æquiores, qui doctrinam Chriſtianam profitentur quidem, ſed parvi pendunt, aut erroribus contaminant: item qui dignitati noſtræ invident, aut poſſeſſionibus inhiant. Quot autem univerſi ſint, quantumque conſociati valeant, animus dicere horreſcit.

Jam porro, ut de Pontificiis taceam, qui occultis licet nunc dierum odiis, immortalibus tamen, diligenter ſibi vires in idoneum tempus comparant; inter ipſos Reformatos, quid de Diſſentientium, uti vocitantur, Fratrum affectu ſtatuemus? Hos quidem ſpes erat in matris antiquæ gremium ſe propediem recepturos; utpote tandem Epiſcopatum & Liturgiam præſcriptam vel probantes, vel ferri poſſe confitentes, nec amplius innocuis cæremoniis, tanquam larvis, exterritos.

Contra

Contra vero nuper illorum plures, partim opiniones pravas de variis Fidei Capitibus arripuerunt, partim hoc nobis objiciunt, quod quæ legibus civilibus fundatur Ecclesia, eo ipso desiit Christo rite subesse. Unde cum prius videri poteramus in mutuos ruituri amplexus, nunc ex improviso resiliunt, diffidentque longissime: nec raro amicitias cum apertis Christiani nominis hostibus studiose colunt, dum nos asperrime exagitant.

Hi igitur omnes, quos hactenus memoravi, statim ut aliquid aggredi cœpimus, cuncta clamoribus opplebunt, aliud Synodum præ se ferre, aliud meditari dictitabunt, affectatæ tyrannidis dicam scribent, patulis multorum auribus, quæ sibi imaginantur, facile infundent; at que etiam quæ ipsi non credunt, aliis persuadebunt. Etenim sunt mire propensi homines, alioquin haud mali, ad suspiciones adversum nos fovendas: quæ cum antehac (nam fatendum est,) aliquatenus justæ fuerint, nimium tenaci reconduntur usque memoria, nec absque diuturno labore eximentur.

Verum obsepta est et aliis obstaculis via. Non adeo multa sane, quod mihi quidem constat,

constat, prompta habemus, quæ in Synodo proponantur: eaque brevi spatio possemus ad exitum perducere. Sed cum primum rumor percrebuerit ad negotia tractanda nos accingi, plurimas illico plurimi molitiones instituent, suum quisque commentum invitis ingerens; mille opinionum obtrudentur monstra, mille speciosæ, aut ne speciosæ quidem, rerum novandarum formulæ, quædam a malevolis, quædam ab indoctis aut rudibus, quædam etiam a cordatioribus ipsis: et quod hic necessarium, ille exitabile esse pronunciabit. Hæc omnia si rejicimus oblata, superbum videbitur: si sumimus dijudicanda, in infinitum res abibit: quoquo nos vertamus, gravem offensionem concitabimus; nec tandem fortasse quidquam decernere, aut si decernimus obtinere ut ratum sit, valebimus. Non sum nescius morem antiquitus fuisse sententiarum varietates Synodorum decretis reprimere: sed cum Synodi, sed cum Clerici separatim, pondus haberent, quo nunc plane carent. Nam hodie quidem plurimis ludus est, immo etiam honori sibi ducant, nos petulanter frustrari, quanquam nec oderint, nec metuant: quod longe acrius aggredientur,

tur, cum intermiſſa diu conſilia renovari intellexerint.

Dicet quis forſan, Regem ſalutis publicæ & fidei Chriſtianæ ſtudioſiſſimum, ſi minus ultro, ſaltem admonitum, certe ornaturum nos rerum conſtituendarum poteſtate, & adverſus improborum machinationes in tuto collocaturum. Et quidem talem ovanti patriæ divinitus contigiſſe ex imo pectore vobis gratulor; Deumque veneror ut poſſit, quod velle ſcio, in Religionis amorem ſuos accendere, & Ordini noſtro debitum honorem conciliare. Sed nec poteſt omnia, nec inopportuno tempore quidpiam adorietur, nec iis inconſultis, quorum ſpecta fide & ſapientia merito nititur. Jam hi, bene quidem nobis volunt, ut nemo poſſit melius: ſed rerum ſuarum, hac præſertim tempeſtate, ſatagunt; & inde noſtris (nam quid apud vos parcam proloqui?) aliquanto minus dedunt ſe, quam optandum eſſet. Metuunt nempe, ne ſi res bellicas eccleſiaſticis cumulent, obruantur negotiorum multitudine. Metuunt etiam, ne quid a nobis, ne quid ſaltem ab aliis, turbetur. Juſto timidiores, vel ſane ſegniores, forſan putabitis, qui talia cauſentur.

Nec intercedo. Habent tamen illa fpeciem aliquam, qua fi capiantur ifti, non eft nimis indignandum. Et dum folenne illud fuum identidem occentant, *quieta non movenda*, mirum ni affentiatur princeps juvenis, magis aliquando fibi nobifque fifurus.

Quin fingamus conceffam, quæ expetitur, facultatem. Si pauca tantum, eaque leviora complecteretur, multi nos magno conatu nihil agere dicerent: et cum vel minimis aliquod tempus dandum fit, noftrûm non exiguus numerus domum pertæfi diliberentur, relicta Synodo infrequente & inhonoratâ. Quod fi multa & gravia demandarentur, alii nihil reftare integrum clamitarent; & poffet evenire, ut in partes ipfi diftraheremur. Spero equidem, & amplam fpei materiam præbet afpectus vefter, fic nos affectos effe, ut ardentiores lenioribus, expertis rerum inexperti, fe vilient fubmittere, nemo temere aut feorfim quidquam inceptare, nemo pertinaciter urgere periculofa vel fufpecta. Sed nefcio an hæc omnia fpondere quis aufit: quæ tamen fi minus præftabimus, quandocunque arceffemur in commune confulturi, opinionum difcrepantiam conflictu incendentur

dentur iræ, fcindemur in ftudia contra, lateque a nobis manabunt in publicum difcordiæ. Hujufmodi multa in civilibus comitiis impune fiunt: in noftris fiebant olim: nunc nemo ferret. Undique incurfarent, undique impeterent nos: nec mora, pro imperio edicerent, qui poffunt, finem hifce diffidiis actutum quoquo modo effe imponendum. Abrumpenda effet repente tela exorfa: conquererentur bonorum non pauci noftra culpa nihil fucceffiffe, fed omnia deteriora facta; & falfe deriderent nos quotquot funt alieni, vel a Chriftiana fide, vel ab hierarchia Anglicana. Quinetiam fi nullæ lites orirentur, eo certius malignitatem & livorem quorundam exftimularemus. Nam qui maxime diffenfionum nos accufant, minime eadem fentire, & bene rem gerere cupiunt.

His de caufis, tametfi prorfus arbitrii noftri effet ad negotia capeffenda ftatim convolare, quid prudentiores exiftimarent, haud dixerim: ego ampliandum cenferem.

Quid ergo? Jubeone vos de Synodo actuofa, deque Ecclefiæ ftatu per eam emendando, defperare? Abfit vero. Semper enitendum

tendum eſt, ut antiqui regiminis non modo retineamus formam, ſed et vim inſtauremus, quatenus vel divino vel humano jure fulcitur. Atque interim manca quodammodo et mutila erit πολιτεια noſtra. Hoc tantum caveri velim, ne, quod fieri, vel tuto fieri, nequit, exoptemus; ne audacibus & calidis inceptis faveamus; ne laqueis implicemur, unde expedire nos erit difficile. Hoc tantum commoneo, lentis paſſibus eſſe procedendum, cuncta circumſpectanda, impedimenta ſedulo amolienda, & ſubſternenda, diligenter meditatæ ſtructuræ firma fundamenta. Non eſt igitur oratio mea procraſtrinantis, eludendi cauſâ, ſed in juſtum tempus differentis. Erit etiam, bona cum venia veſtra, præcipientis quo pacto maturabitur quod avemus.

Permagni ad hoc propoſitum intereſt, ut ſimus ipſi, quoſque paſcimus greges efficiamus, quantum res patitur, unanimes, potiſſimum in fide ſalutari. Sunt enim qui ſe noſtros vocant, nihilo tamen ſecius multa quæ docemus improbant; ſpeciatim, quæ ad S. S. Trinitatem pertinent, ad Redemptionem generis humani, ad illapſum Gratiæ cæleſtis in mentes fidelium. Jam vero ſi longius

longius proserpserit error sententiam de his receptam repudiantium; vel si invalescant qui comminiscuntur, præter horum persuasionem, bonorum operum feracem, necessariam esse fiduciam favoris apud Deum, sensibus imis infixam superne, quæ omnem dubitationem tollat : controversiis assiduis vexabimur; ad Synodos cum effectu celebrandas, *non in melius,* ut Apostoli verbis utar, *sed in deterius conveniemus*[b]. Nec solum conquassabitur, tandemque dissolvetur hujus Ecclesiæ pulcherrima compages; quin etiam corrumpetur integritas vitalis doctrinæ, siquidem ego, diu perpensis & subductis, ancipiti quondam animo, rationibus, verum discernere valeo.

Sunt autem porro, qui se minime de Fide a nobis dissentire, aut affirmant, aut videri volunt, sed æquum censent omnibus placita quæcunque propugnantibus ad mensam eucharisticam, atque adeo ad sacros ordines, aditum patere, modo in Christum se credere profiteantur. Sed hoc professi sunt olim Hæreticorum pestilentissimi: ne dicam hodie quadantenus profiteri Mohammedanos. Ad-

[b] 1 Cor. xi. 17.

mittantur

mittantur ergo, aiunt, ii foli, qui facras fcripturas venerantur, ejufque verbis animorum fenfa declarare funt parati. Quid vero? Pontificii, Tremulorum fecta, innumerarum ineptiarum fautores, nonne in id funt parati? Hofne ergo omnes honore fungendi apud nos Sacerdotii dignantur? Sin minus; cur alios, pari ratione repellendos?

Verum hoc faltem Candidatis urgent concedendum, ut fuis, non alienis verbis fatisfaciant Ecclefiæ Rectoribus: quod et antiquitus ufu veniffe monent. Atque ita fæpe diuque factum non negamus; fed idcirco, & merito quidem, fieri defiiffe credimus, quod fic Epifcoporum quifque, vel oratione fubdola, cui difcutiendæ fpatium non effet, facile falli potuerit, vel pro arbitrio recte fentientibus viam intercludere, prava fentientes admittere: quodque hinc neceffe fuerit frequenter evenire, ut eundem hic refpueret, ille amplecteretur, et difceptandis litibus inde oriundis una Synodus haud fufficeret.

Efto igitur, idoneos Articulos Fidei in auxilium vocandos: at certe noftros recoquendos, & incudi reddendos, non pauci contendent.

contendent. Nec diffitemur potuisse quædam aptius enunciari, et adversus tam argutias quam hallucinationes melius muniri. Sed præclare, ut illis temporibus, instructa & composita sunt omnia: egentque hodie tantum explicatione commoda: non vafram & veteratoriam intelligo, sed artis grammaticæ criticæque regulis consonam. Nec leve est periculum, ne qui, integris manentibus Articulis, nos ab eorum vera mente descivisse jactitant, ἑτεροδοξίας crimen atrociori longe clamore, tristiorique eventu impingant, si medicas iis manus, tanquam malesanis, adhibeamus.

Et hæc eadem velim sibi in memoriam revocent, qui Liturgiam item recenseri reformarique flagitant. Ornatior quidem, accuratior, plenior, brevior, et potest ea fieri & debet: sed modesta tractatione, sed tranquillis hominum animis; non temerariis, qualia vidimus & videmus, ausis, non inter media diffidia, mutuasque suspiciones.

Verum ut de his statuatur, novam saltem Scripturæ versionem desiderari, plurimis videtur: nempe ut populus Christianus ea luce fruatur, quæ favente Numine oraculis divinis

per

per continuas virorum doctorum vigilias affulsit, hisce 150 annis proxime elapsis, ante quos confecta est Anglica Vulgata. Et quis refragetur honestissimæ petitioni? Sed ad hoc opus post conquisitum undique omnigenæ eruditionis apparatum demum accedendum est; atque in eo versandum summa religione, cautela, industria, cura porro inter multos amicissime conspirantes, per longum tempus, dispertita. Prodeunt quotidie certatim interpretes: sed fere proletarii, vel quorum supervacanea diligentia incertiores multo sumus quam dudum. Revivicit linguæ sanctæ perquam necessaria cognitio: sed justas vires nondum acquisivit, & somniis suis se oblectant quidam ejus cultores. Expectandum ideo, si aliquid operâ dignum facere volumus, donec hi aut resipuerint, aut erroris manifesti sint, donec deferbuerit novorum sensuum eruendorum æstus, & nupera hæc pene dixeram rabies emendandi, qua impelluntur ut mendis imprudenter referciant codicem sacrum homines probi, nec ineruditi; donec denique exitum aliquem habeat laudandum apprime institutum conferendi inter se, & cum primævis interpretationibus,

bus, Veteris Testamenti libros Hebraice scriptos.

Ego sane in omnibus, de quibus dixi, labores vel maximos, quantum patitur ingravescens & jam fere præceps ætas, pro Ecclesiæ bono, non detrectem, nec offensiones reformidem. Sed minime velim eorum suscipiendorum auctor esse, unde magis gliscant nimiæ jampridem rixæ. Nam his vigentibus protelabitur usque Synodi conventus efficax, ne nobis permissi bella intestina suscitemus, publicis commodis nocitura. Quod si semel satis concordes videamur, minuetur iste, qui penitus, quanquam injuria, in virorum summorum animis insedit, metus: quem et omnino depulsum fore sperari potest, modo palam faciamus nos in omnes, utcunque diversa sentientes, benevole animatos esse, ut quidem sumus. Quotusquisque enim est nostrum, quin hanc rem sic secum reputet?
" Errat quispiam; mirum ni et ego: sed
" aut vocabulo tantum, aut si re, innoxie.
" Errat vehementer: sed non continuo est
" Hæreticus. Hæreticus est: sed Christia-
" nus tamen. Ne Christianus quidem: sed
" Homo saltem. Homo malus forsitan:
" sed

" sed qui poterit in melius mutari. Fac
" denique non posse: Deus vindicabit."
Nec idcirco aut flagitiis inquinati, aut sanorum verborum formulæ pertinaciter adversantes, non sunt a cœtu piorum segregandi. Sed in mitiorem partem, tum dictis, tum factis, est propendendum: nec eadem nobis homuncionibus, quæ Apostolis falli nesciis fuit, auctoritas arroganda est. Etenim longe tutius erit sinere ut zizania tantisper cum tritico succrescant, quam eos ejicere, quos tandem Judex communis, magno cum nostro dedecore, postliminio restituet. Et qui severius agi postulant, imbecillitatis suæ sunt immemores: nec vident quod est apertissimum, hac via periculose concussum, forsan etiam eversum, iri, quam stabilitum eunt Ecclesiam.

Nec tamen, ut gaudeamus tranquillitate, rerum theologicarum studia sunt remittenda: sed excitanda ex diuturno quo languent torpore. Non est hæc ætas nostra legendis, præsertim antiquioribus, aut gravioris argumenti, libris, nedum attentæ cogitationi, vel scriptioni operosæ, satis dedita. Olim tractatibus omnium generum, doctrina,

judicio,

judicio, acumine confpicuis, inclaruimus: nunc non exaruit quidem, fed arefcit, uberrimus ille laudum fons. Olim contra Infideles, Pontificios, oppugnatores quofcunque, fumma cum gloria militavimus: quorum venenatis voluminibus, domi forifque affatim editis, nunc parum aut nihil reponimus: unde illis famæ celebritas, & difcipulorum multitudo; nobis opprobium. Nec utique exiftimabitur illos, quorum pauci quidquam feparatim præftant, multum præftituros in Synodum convocatos. Video quid poffit obtendi: & fponte fateor, profpiciendum effe, nam concreditum eft, nobis qui dicimur Beneficiorum Patroni, ne eruditæ diligentiæ præmia defint. Dandum fane aliquid hac in re, ut in omnibus, cognationi, honeftis minifteriis, precibus amicorum, potentiorum commendationibus, juffa verius vocaverim: fed nullatenus tantum, ut vel mali, vel plane inhabiles, admittantur ad facra munia, vel neglecti jaceant boni & litterati. Quod utinam plures fe exhiberent, qui ftudiis recte pofitis, et eorum fructibus in lucem prolatis, omnem nobis excufationem præriperent, fi quando in minus merentes largius æquo fimus benefici.

Quanto autem quis eft vel doctrina ornatior, vel conditione fuperior, tanto oportebit, hoc potiffimum fæculo, ut fe gerat fubmiffius. Officii paftoralis dignitatem, in qua conftituti fumus, affidue fufpicere & tueri debemus: verum fi amplificare aggredimur infcite, imminuemus non mediocriter. Neque ecclefiaftica, neque civilia, quibus potimur, abjudicare jura, aut licet aut expedit: nam qui illis nofmet ultro exuentes collaudare nos non definent, exutos ridebunt. Sed fi juftam auctoritatem confervare volumus, ante omnia cavendum eft, ne immodicam vindicemus. Alioquin magis atque magis in auguftum coercebimur: et demum exilis illa, quæ reftat, umbra regiminis eripietur, fumma cum plurimorum afpernatione.

Nec indecore appetentes erimus (modo fapere, et bene audire, atque adhiberi feriis negotiis cordi eft) aut dulcis lucelli, aut gradus cujuflibet altioris. Non funt, experto credite, non funt tanti vel honores vel reditus ampliffimi Ecclefiafticis deftinati,

ut

ut à quopiam enixe cupiantur. Multum habent follicitudinis, non parum forfan invidiæ; vere delectationis nihil, nifi quoties occurrit, occurrit autem raro infignis, benefaciendi occafio.

Voluptates, etiam honeftiores, parcè ufurpare, nec a vituperandis tantummodo, fed à contemnendis vel parvi faciendis, abftinere fe, ad exiftimationem Clericorum intereft quam maxime. Si quos è nobis videant Laici, potionum & ciborum lautitiis indulgentes, corporis cultui & veftium elegantiæ præter modum addictos, in facetias & rifum perpetuo folutos, muliercularum chartis luforiis continenter inhiantium circulis & feffiunculis permixtos, vel inter quafcunque nugas inerti otio fugaces horas difperdentes, nunquam fe perfuaderi finent, ut ex frequentiffimo talium concilio boni quidpiam proficifci poffe fperent: quales tamen fi aliquot noftrûm comperiant, cæteros ejufdem effe farinæ libenter fibi fingent.

Sed minime fatis erit vitam agere cætera inculpatam, nifi in docendo quoque Evangelio, quod munus eft noftrum, parvi & ampli gnaviter elaboremus. Quo effrænatius luxuriantur

luxuriantur errores & vitia, quo laxior est Ecclesiæ disciplina, quo lenior administratio Reipublicæ, eo diligentiorem adhiberi oportet in fide & præceptis Christianis institutionem: & incassum ad industriam hortabimur Sacerdotes inferioris ordinis, nisi exemplo præeamus. Potuimus non ita pridem impetrare, ut delinquentes in bonos mores Magistratui pœnas darent; ut libri impii & impudici e medio tollerentur: nunc illud ægre conceditur; hoc sciens loquor, neutiquam. Est ideo vel sola vi argumentorum, præsertim in sacris Concionibus, obsistendum adversariis, vel cedendum loco. Et cum præter adversarios veteres, novi & domestici nuper ex ipso Academiarum nostratium sinu profiluerint, qui se solos æternæ salutis tramitem commonstrare, nos in perniciem cæcorum more evagari, passim prædicant, curatissime dispiciendum est, ut recto cursu veritatis viam insistamus; horum nec astutiis illecti, nec timore perculsi, nec odio flagrantes: cavendum, ne, si illi sermones suos ad vulgi captum nimis accommodant, ac demittunt, nos hoc nimis dedignemur; ne, si illi sunt justo vehementiores, nos

frigidi

frigidi videamur, & affectuum piorum expertes; ne si illi efficaciam Fidei immoderatè cum maximo fidelium periculo extollunt, nos non minori ingrate eam deprimamus & extenuemus; ne si illi inania visa & phantasmata pro certis pignoribus Remissionis Peccatorum habent, nos in genuinum Spiritus Sancti testimonium simus imprudenter contumeliosi.

Egone igitur Clerum Anglicanum officii vel male intellecti, vel male præstiti, tecte insimulo? Deus meliora. Quî potest ut vituperem quos diligo & revereor; quorum plurimorum, cum vita functorum tum superstitum, amicitia diu gavisus sum; & exempla mihi quotidie ob oculos pono, ut ad recte vivendum docendumque me erigam & confirmem? Sed vos auditoribus vestris, etiamsi summa laude dignis, monitiones tamen sollicite ingeritis. Nam vel sapientes Virgines dormitâsse legimus [c]: *thesaurum evangelicum in vasis fictilibus habemus* [d]: & difficile est à moribus hodiernis aliquid contagionis & labis non trahere. Ignoscat Pater misericors, quod Parœciis primo, de-

[c] Matth. xxv. 5.   [d] 2 Cor. iv. 7.

inde Dioecefibus mihi ordine commiffis, minus intente & perite, quam oportuerat, invigilaverim! Ignofcat pariter, fi quid fimile cuiquam veftrum contigerit! Illud autem ftatuamus univerfi, aucto follicite ftudio, compenfare pro virili (nunquam enim fiet fatis,) quicquid peccavimus: idque eo certe potiffimum, ut nos Deo commendemus; partim vero etiam, ut hominibus.

Neque enim ferent in Clericis illa, quorum facile fibi invicem dant veniam. Quod fi *nobis & doctrinæ*, ex Apoftoli præcepto, *attendamus* [e]; nequit fieri, quin gradatim in altum recrefcat exiftimatio noftra; quin perfpiciant quotidie clarius quibus rerum habenæ funt traditæ, quot quantifque in rebus operâ noftrâ uti poffunt; quin tandem non modo concedant, verum & Reipublicæ caufa invitent rogentque, ut quæ Ecclefiæ defunt communi confilio fuppleamus. Longa quidem eft hæc via atque ardua: fed eft ea quæ volumus, aut velle debemus, unica; & quas fortaffe indicabunt alii compendarias, in falebrofos ducunt & præcipites locos. His artibus flo-

[e] 1 Tim. iv. 16.

ruerunt

ruerunt primorum fæculorum Doctores: his iifdem nobis fidendum eft: aliarum ope non dabitur in honore effe: vel fi maxime daretur, aliarum ope nec inferviremus hominum utilitati, nec æternum vitam confequeremur.

Tarde & cunctuanter credo, quicquid faciemus, de nobis honorificè plerique fentient. Iracundæ tamen querimoniæ multum aberit ut proficiant; quorundam animos malevolo gaudio perfundent; alios movebunt, ut quos contemnunt, etiam oderint. Accufati vicifsim accufabunt: & coram iniquis judicibus caufa nobis erit dicenda. Nec fane proderit vehemens negotiorum civilium tractandorum ftudium confpiciendum dare. Ferventiorem enim hancce cupiditatem, ad privata fpectare emolumena, non ad communia, perhibebunt fufpicaces & maligni, vulgus credet. Quæ noftra funt ergo rite peragentes, eventum, quem daturus eft Deus, tranquille expectemus. Viros bonos colamus, quamvis minime nobifcum in omnibus confentiant: impiis ne focii quidem fimus, nedum adulatores; nec tamen temere offenfiones demus, fed neceffariam reprehenfionum in jucunditatem verborum humanitate mitigemus:

mus: modicum aliis non inviti permittamus illorum ufum, licita modo fint, quæ ipfi non attingimus: ab omni concertatione longiffime abhorreamus: injurias & opprobia toleranter patiamur: favore, ex quacunque demum parte affulferit, utamur modefte. Hoc modo nec novas contrahemus inimicitias, & majorum delicta aut non luemus amplius, aut luemus immeriti.

In utramque idcirco partem parati fimus. Rerum facrarum, &, quotquot aliquo vinculo cum his connexæ funt, civilium, fcientia fic nos inftruamus, quafi brevi effemus de quæftionibus graviffimis deliberationes habituri: compofiti tamen interim ad fummam æquitatem & manfuetudinem, fi vel in longiffimum diem fpes illa prorogetur: qua fi penitus fruftremur, dolebimus quidem fæculi, male & fibi confulentis, & nobis gratiam referentis, five iniquitatem five incogitantiam: hoc vero noftrâ culpa non obtigiffe, toto pectore lætabimur; nec fpernendum nihilominus per nos incrementum capiet res Chriftiana. In Synodo fententiam non dicemus: fed feorfim conftanter quod verum atque decens propugnabimus. Canones non condemus:

condemus: sed ut omnes omnia sua ad Canonem Sacri Fœderis exigant, tam verbis quam exemplo suadebimus. Anathematum fulminibus heterodoxes non feriemus: (atque utinam ab odiosis ejusmodi & appellationibus & inceptis temperavissent sibi Decessores nostri:) sed *cum modestia*, Divino Paulo edicente, *corripiemus eos qui resistunt, ne quando Deus det illis pœnitentiam ad cognoscendam veritatem* [f]. In Clericos vitiis contaminatos aut vecordes non exercebimus communiter censuram: sed ne locum inveniant apud nos, cura privata quantum licet præcavebimus. Libros infames carbone haud notabimus, unde avidius legerentur; sed accurate refellemus. Et quamvis dubio careret, indies imminutam his in oris atque tandem extinctam, fore cælestem Evangelii lucem: illachrymandum quidem esset popularibus nostris misere pereuntibus; in voluntate tamen divina non gravatim acquiescendum. Quid enim Propheta? *In vacuum laboravi, & vane fortitudinem meam consumpsi: ergo judicium meum cum Domino, & opus meum cum Deo meo* [g].

[f] 2 Tim. ii. 25.   [g] Esai. xlix. 4.

Condonate mihi, Patres Fratresque, longi hujus alloquii tædium; ex hac Cathedra nunc primum, nunc itidem postremum, (sic enim præsagit mens, & verisimile est) vos compellanti. *Tuque, omnipotens & sempiterne Deus, cujus Spiritu universum Ecclesiæ corpus regitur sanctumque efficitur, supplicationes & preces nostras, pro cujuscunque ordinis hominibus, qui in Ecclesiam tuam cooptantur, oblatas tibi admitte; ut quisque, sicut suæ convenit vocationi & ministerio, tibi sincere & pie serviat, per Dominum & Servatorem nostrum Jesum Christum. Amen*[h].

---

[h] Collect. 2. Parascev.

FINIS.

www.ingramcontent.com/pod-product-compliance
Lightning Source LLC
Chambersburg PA
CBHW030401230426
43664CB00007BB/695